THE SUPER BOOK OF BASEBALL

THE SUPER BOOK
OF BASEBALL

Ron Berler

A *Sports Illustrated For Kids* Book

First Edition

Library of Congress Cataloging-in-Publication Data
Berler, Ron.
    The super book of baseball / Ron Berler.—1st ed.
      p. cm
    "A Sports illustrated for kids book."
    Summary: Surveys the history of baseball, from its origins
and early years to the most recent World Series.
    ISBN 0-316-09240-1
    1. Baseball—United States—History—Juvenile literature.
2. Baseball—United States—Records—Juvenile literature.
[1. Baseball—History.] I. Title
GV863.A1B471991
796.357'0973—dc20   90-46568

SPORTS ILLUSTRATED FOR KIDS is a trademark of
THE TIME INC. MAGAZINE COMPANY

Sports Illustrated For Kids Books is a joint imprint of Little,
Brown and Company and Warner Juvenile Books. This title is
published in arrangement with Cloverdale Press Inc.

10 9 8 7 6 5 4 3 2 1

WOR

For further information regarding this title, write to Little, Brown
and Company, 34 Beacon Street, Boston, MA 02108

Published simultaneously in Canada by Little Brown & Company
(Canada)

Printed in the United States of America

Interior design by Charlotte Staub

CONTENTS

Introduction vii

Section 1: HISTORY

1 Baseball's Origins and Early
   Years 3
2 The Modern Years 18
3 Baseball's Greatest and Goofiest
   Plays and Streaks 26
4 Time Line 37

Section 2: THE PLAYERS

5 Today's Big Names 51
6 Hall of Fame Players 64
7 The Greatest Teams of All Time 76

Section 3: AROUND THE LEAGUES

8 The Teams of the National
   League 87
9 The Teams of the American
   League 97

Section 4: TALKIN' BASEBALL

10 All-Time Record Holders and
   World Series Winners 111
11 Baseball Nicknames 121

Glossary 127

Dedication

Thank you, Duke Snider, for the years when you were my hero.
Thank you, Tom Willis, John Fink and Larry Townsend for being my first guardian angels.
Thank you, Ron King, for suggesting me for this project.
Thank you, Don D'Auria, for asking me to write it.
Thank you, Rick Telander, for believing in me.

For all my Little Leaguers, past and future; for my brothers, Randy and Richard; and, most of all, for my mother.

INTRODUCTION

Dr. Barzun is an educator and historian who came from France to the United States in 1919, when he was 12 years old. How did he learn to fit in, to make friends? Through the one common language—baseball—that nearly every American speaks.

There are a thousand games in a hundred countries in which the object is to toss or kick or hit a ball and try to score, but none is so perfect as this one. None is so democratic. Are you short and skinny? Shaped like an egg-plant? It doesn't matter, there's a place for you to play. Baseball is the rare team sport where size doesn't matter, where every one of us can dream of making the majors.

Baseball was probably the first sport you learned to play. The first time you played catch with your mom or dad was probably with a baseball, not a basketball or football. The first stadium you visited was likely a major league ballpark. The first cards you collected were undoubtedly baseball cards. The first team you cheered for was probably your favorite baseball team.

Baseball is rooted in your heart. You are lucky. You will spend your entire life in love with this game. Talk to your mom or dad. They're a lot older than you, but you may find that baseball has the same hold on them that it has on you.

I could go on, but my friends are calling from the other room. The commercial is over, and the announcer is reading the starting lineups on TV. He says the Cubs can win it all, if their stars can stay healthy and they can find another starting pitcher. Maybe this will be the year. Here comes the first pitch. I have to run.

Play ball!

CHAPTER 1

BASEBALL'S ORIGINS AND EARLY YEARS

WHO INVENTED BASEBALL? NO, IT WASN'T ABNER DOUBLEDAY

Abner Doubleday, you say, invented baseball. You've read about him in books. Everybody knows his name. According to legend, he laid out the first ball field in 1839, in Elihu Phinney's Cooperstown cow pasture, not far from the current site of the Baseball Hall of Fame.

Strike three, game's over, you're out!

Doubleday was many things—a heroic Civil War general, a talented writer, a gripping public speaker. There is no evidence, however, that he wrote or lectured about baseball or even knew how to play the game.

That didn't matter to a special baseball commission appointed in 1907 "to determine the origins of the great American pastime." The members of the commission were out to prove that baseball was a purely American invention, and that it was in no way related to a somewhat similar English game called "rounders." Ignoring all evidence to the contrary, they named Doubleday as the game's

sole creator. The general died in 1893, so he was unable to protest.

Until very recently, the real inventor of baseball—as we know it—was thought to be a 25-year-old New York bank clerk and volunteer fireman named Alexander Cartwright. In 1845, in a Manhattan public park, he introduced his adaptation of rounders. He set four bases in a diamond shape, 90 feet apart. He placed the batter at home plate, instead of several feet away, toward first, as in rounders. He limited the number of outfielders to three, and invented a new position he called "short stop." Fielders were to throw to bases to make outs, instead of throwing at the base runners. He drew foul lines. In rounders, an entire team had to be retired to end an inning, but

Alexander Cartwright, once thought to be the real inventor of baseball.

3

One of the first baseball games, played in 1846.

Cartwright reduced the outs needed to complete an inning to three. Later, he conceived the nine-inning game. In 1846, two teams met on the Elysian Fields in Hoboken, New Jersey, and played the first game with Cartwright's rules. But the earliest known report of a baseball game, referred to as "the time-honored game of Base," was published on October 21, 1845. So it looks like Mr. Cartwright didn't invent it, either.

YOU WOULDN'T RECOGNIZE THE EARLY RULES

Over the next 23 years, amateur teams blossomed in towns and cities across America. Some communities took losing better than others. In 1867, after a barnstorming team called the Washington (D.C.) Nationals beat the Cincinnati Red Stockings, Cincinnatians swore revenge. They hired a bunch of ringers—the first professional ballplayers. Harry Wright, a local jeweler and amateur player, was paid $1,200 to manage and play centerfield for the Red Stockings. Only one other player came from Cincinnati.

The Red Stockings were not perfect, but they were close. They played 57 games and won 56—and tied the other one. Team president Aaron Champion announced he would rather be president of the Red Stockings than President of the United States.

That wasn't true a year later. The club unexpectedly lost to a Brooklyn team, and other defeats quickly followed. When the players demanded bigger salaries, Champion disbanded the team.

Clubs and leagues came and went until 1876, when Chicago businessman William A. Hulbert and seven other owners created the National League. In 1901, a competing group of owners created the rival American League. Initially, the two leagues didn't exactly get along. In 1904, the National League champion New York Giants refused to play the American League champion Boston Pilgrims in the World Series.

At least the two leagues did agree on the rules. During the 1880s, the rules had changed nearly every year. In 1879, it took nine balls to draw a walk. A year later, it took eight. It dropped to seven in 1881, to six in 1884, went back to seven in 1886, down to five in 1887, and finally to four in 1889. During this time, the pitching distance was moved back from 45 feet to 50 feet, and in 1893 to the present 60 feet, 6 inches. For a brief period, flat bats were legal. Until 1887, batters could request high or low pitches.

John McGraw, manager of
the rowdy New York Giants.

The Giants Hall of Fame
pitcher, Christy Mathewson.

BASEBALL'S FIRST DYNASTY

The two leagues reached peace in 1905, and the sport's first great dynasty emerged six years later—John McGraw's New York Giants. McGraw was a rough, brawling, street-smart manager, and his teams reflected his personality. The Giants, except for gentlemanly Hall of Fame pitcher Christy Mathewson, were a collection of rowdy, spikes-in-the-air toughs who intimidated their way to victory. The 1911 Giants led the league with a record 347 stolen bases. That same season, Mathewson and fellow Hall of Famer Rube Marquard won 50 games between them. McGraw's Giants won 10 pennants in 21 years.

Baseball had become a profitable business by the early part of the century—so profitable that in 1914 a third league, the Federal League, declared itself a major league, and began buying star ballplayers from the National and American Leagues. The Federal League lasted two seasons before it shut down. There have been just two major leagues ever since.

The 1911 Giants bullied their way to the top.

The 1919 "Black Sox" team.

THE BLACK SOX SCANDAL

Baseball had become the national sport by 1919, but, in truth, fans didn't put much trust in the game. For years, there had been rumors that gamblers had fixed the outcome of some games. Then, in 1919, the heavily favored Chicago White Sox—a truly great team with three Hall of Famers and two other players who might have made it to Cooperstown—somehow lost to the Cincinnati Reds in the World Series. Losing a game is nothing to be ashamed of, but it seemed as if the White Sox had lost on purpose.

Two years later, eight of the White Sox—outfielders "Shoeless" Joe Jackson and Oscar "Happy" Felsch, pitchers Eddie Cicotte and Claude Williams, first baseman Chick Gandil, shortstop Swede Risberg, third baseman Buck Weaver and utility man Fred McMullin—were tried in a Chicago court. The charge: The players had accepted $100,000 from gamblers, who told them to intentionally lose the 1919 World Series. The nation was shocked. People felt betrayed. How could their heroes have done such a thing? The White Sox became popularly known as the Black Sox, and all of baseball was hurt by the scandal.

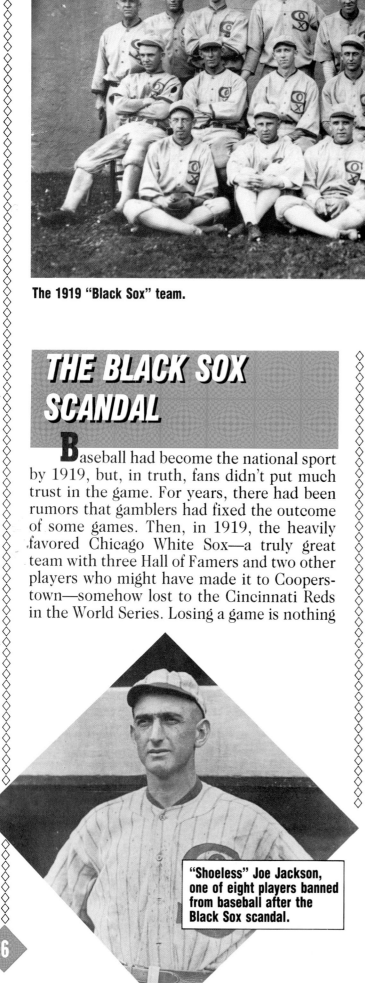

"Shoeless" Joe Jackson, one of eight players banned from baseball after the Black Sox scandal.

Baseball's first commissioner, Kenesaw Mountain Landis.

The owners, fearful that the game was in danger of being destroyed, hired the sport's first commissioner in hopes of cleaning it up. They chose a tough, moralistic federal judge named Kenesaw Mountain Landis. The court found the players innocent because of a lack of hard evidence, but that wasn't good enough for Landis. After all, all of the players except Buck Weaver took the cash. Landis banned all eight players from the game for life.

THE YANKEES DYNASTY

While Landis's strong leadership slowly won back the trust of the fans, it took a larger-than-life young slugger named George Herman "Babe" Ruth to win their hearts. In 1917, New York Yankees first baseman Wally Pipp led the American League with nine home runs. Three years later, Ruth, the Yankees wide-nosed, barrel-chested, spindle-legged rightfielder, smashed an unbelievable 54 home runs. He hit more home runs than any American League *team* other than the Yan-

kees. The following season, 1921, he hit 59. In 1927, Babe hit 60 homers, setting a record that would stand for 34 years.

Before Ruth, baseball had been a game of singles, stolen bases and hit-and-run plays. The Babe changed the very way the sport was played. Fans were amazed by his power, and they swarmed to Yankee Stadium to watch him hit. Owners of other teams were quick to cash in on Ruth's popularity by introducing a livelier baseball (one that went farther when you hit it) and seeking home run hitters for their own clubs. The Cardinals signed Rogers Hornsby (who hit 301 career home runs and had a .358 lifetime average), the Athletics found Jimmie Foxx (534 homers) and Al Simmons (307), the Giants brought up Mel Ott (511) and the Cubs traded for Hack Wilson (56 home runs in 1930). No team, though, could hit like the New York Yankees. Lou Gehrig (493 homers) joined the team in 1923. The Yankees, with Babe Ruth leading the way, won six pennants during the Roaring Twenties.

By the 1930s, the Yankees were a team of elegance, of style, of tradition. Almost every kid who dreamed of playing baseball dreamed of being a Yankee. They played in a cathedral-

Lou Gehrig helped the Yankees win six pennants during the 1920s.

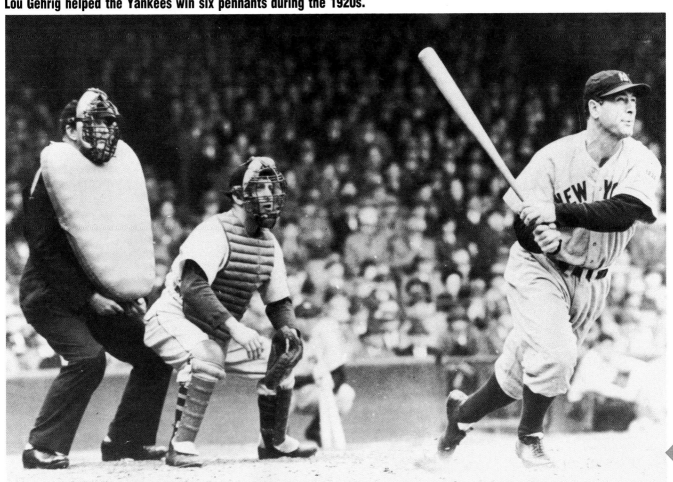

The Yankees Babe Ruth smashed home runs like no one had ever seen before.

like ballpark and dressed in distinctive pin-striped uniforms. They were the best, and it showed. Watching the Yankees was fun and impressive, but it wasn't crazy.

THE GASHOUSE GANG

For crazy, you had to go to St. Louis, where Cardinals games sometimes resembled today's World Wrestling Federation matches. One of their pitchers was nicknamed Dizzy. Another—Dizzy's brother—was nicknamed Daffy. Their third baseman, Pepper Martin, was known as "The Wild Hoss of the Osage." He was a pure wild man. He didn't wear socks, and he belly flopped into every base until he looked as if he'd been rolling in the dirt.

In fact, he wasn't too different from anyone else on the 1934 St. Louis team, known to its fans as the Gashouse Gang. "Dizzy" was Jay Hanna Dean, one of the greatest pitchers in the history of the game. In 1934, he won 30 games and lost only 7. His brother, Paul "Daffy" Dean had a pretty good season also, going 19–11. At shortstop was Leo "The Lip" Durocher, a man whose mouth never rested. The second baseman and manager, who matched Durocher scream for scream, was Hall of Famer Frankie Frisch.

They were called the Gashouse Gang because they were the loudest, wildest, most colorful, most wrong-side-of-the-tracks ball team ever assembled. But for that one year, they were also the best. They beat the Tigers in the World Series, four games to three, with Dizzy and Daffy each winning twice.

THE FIRST NIGHT GAME

The players weren't the game's only showmen. The owners were like circus barkers, willing to try almost any promotion to lure fans to their ballparks. The most innovative promoter in the game was Cincinnati Reds general manager Larry MacPhail. In 1935, he erected light towers at Crosley Field and hosted the first night game in the major leagues. Night games made it easier for fans who worked during the day to get out to the stadium.

The Reds were hardly the first professional ball team to play under lights. The Des Moines Demons of the old Class A Western League had hosted night games since 1930. By the start of the 1932 season, 13 of the 17 minor

The 1934 St. Louis Cardinals, also known as the Gashouse Gang.

The first night game played at Crosley Field.

leagues played night baseball. On May 24, 1935, the evening the Reds hosted the Phillies, 20,422 fans turned out for the event.

Three years later MacPhail jumped to the Brooklyn Dodgers, where he made Ebbets Field the second lighted ballpark in the major leagues. Brooklyn's first home night game was June 15, 1938, against Cincinnati. Reds pitcher Johnny Vander Meer celebrated the occasion by pitching his second consecutive no-hitter, something no one else has ever accomplished.

By 1941, 11 of the 16 major league clubs had installed lights. The last holdout, the Chicago Cubs, waited 47 more years before it put in lights. The Cubs finally hit the light switch on August 8, 1988.

Other owners looked at the Cubs P.K. Wrigley as a hopeless traditionalist, but in many ways he was a baseball visionary. It was Wrigley who promoted Ladies Day as a way of attracting women to the ballpark. (On Ladies Day, female fans were let in to the park for a reduced price.) And it was Wrigley, in 1943, who started a new league.

WARTIME BASEBALL

After the United States entered World War II at the end of 1941, Wrigley saw that all the best baseball players were leaving their teams and joining the armed services. The Cubs owner feared that the war would shut down baseball and put him out of business. That spring he ordered his team's top scouts to round up the best 200 women softball players in the country. He hoped his All-American Girls Professional Baseball League would fill stadiums until the major leaguers returned from the war.

Wrigley signed 64 women. He divided them into four teams, and shipped them off to Rockford, Illinois; South Bend, Indiana; and Kenosha and Racine, Wisconsin, to play out the league's 108-game schedule.

The new league was an immediate success. The league expanded to 10 teams. The game these women played was good old country hardball. They threw knockdown pitches and charged the shortstop on the double play.

They jawed with umpires, played while injured and were tossed out of games. Millions paid to see them play.

How good were they? After watching shortstop Dorothy Schroeder of the South Bend Blue Sox, Cubs manager Charlie Grimm said, "If she was a boy, I'd give $50,000 for her." Even after the war ended, people still came to the women's games. The league lasted 12 years, before finally closing in 1954.

JACKIE ROBINSON JOINS BROOKLYN

When the players returned home from the war, they found that women players weren't the only addition to baseball. In the spring of 1946, Dodgers president Branch Rickey took the first step toward righting a serious wrong in baseball. He signed black shortstop Jackie Robinson to a minor league contract. A year later, in 1947, Robinson was promoted to the Dodgers, becoming the first black in this century to play major league ball.

That's right—this *century*. In the 1880s, as many as 20 blacks played in the minor leagues. And two blacks—Moses "Fleet" Walker and his brother, Welday—played in 1884 for Toledo, which was then a major league team.

Resentment over the black ballplayers grew both in and out of the leagues, and by 1898 there was an unwritten agreement among baseball owners to ban blacks from the game.

World War II led to the formation of the All-American Girls Professional Baseball League.

Jackie Robinson, the first black player to break the major league color barrier in this century.

However, that did not stop blacks from playing baseball—major-league-quality baseball. Since blacks were not allowed to play on the white teams, they organized their own teams and leagues. Each summer these teams barnstormed thousands of miles by train and by car, to big cities and small towns, criss-crossing the country, challenging any local team that would play them to a game. They traveled with 10 or 11 players, sometimes with no more than two pitchers, and played every day—sometimes several times a day. Later, they organized leagues and played a full schedule of league contests each summer.

The best teams—the Homestead (Pittsburgh) Grays, the Kansas City Monarchs, the Pittsburgh Crawfords—boasted stars as great as any in the major leagues. Catcher Josh Gibson was known as the black Babe Ruth. Pitcher Satchel Paige was the equal of Bob Feller.

Fans knew about these great black players, and major league players did, too. Negro League All-Star games drew as many as 50,000 to Chicago's Comiskey Park. In the off-seasons, black teams played white All-Star teams. Often, the black teams would defeat the white squads. Jackie Robinson played for the Kansas City Monarchs in 1945. He was a wonderful player, but he was not even the best player on his team, let alone in the league. Rickey selected him to break the color line as much for his intelligence and strength of character as for his playing ability. The first black, Rickey knew, would be subjected all season to vicious racial abuse—both from fans and players.

Robinson's first major league season was terrifying at times. He played first base, and opposing players routinely tried to spike him, deliberately sliding into him spikes first. Pitchers threw at his head. The mail brought death threats. But not only did Robinson survive, he flourished. He won the Rookie of the Year Award in 1947, scoring 125 runs, leading the league in stolen bases with 29, batting .297 and leading the Dodgers to the pennant. His struggle opened the door for all the blacks who have played in the major leagues since then.

THE KIDS JOIN THE FUN

In the late 1940s, still another baseball league blossomed. Little League baseball swept the nation. A few years after Carl Stotz, a worker in a sandpaper plant in Williamsport, Pennsylvania, conceived the idea of an organized children's baseball league, Little League had spread to virtually every state in the nation.

In 1947, a team from Williamsport became the first team to win the Little League World Series when it beat Lock Haven, Pennsylvania, 16–7. In 1953, Milwaukee Braves pitcher Joey Jay became the first Little League graduate to play in the major leagues. In 1974, following much debate, girls were allowed to play in Little League. In 1989, the Little League World Series drew 35,000 fans.

Little League first swept the nation in the 1940s.

THE 1950s YANKEES

One thing is clear about the Little League World Series—every year produced a new winner. But watching American League baseball was like watching a bad mystery. You always knew how it would turn out in the end. You knew the Yankees were going to win.

The Yankees, behind Hall of Famers Joe DiMaggio, Mickey Mantle, Yogi Berra and Whitey Ford, won five straight world championships from 1949 to 1953. They finished second in 1954, despite winning 103 games, and then added outfielder Elston Howard and pitcher Bob Turley. This team won the pennant in 1955, the World Series in 1956, the pennant in 1957, and the World Series again in 1958. The Yankees slipped all the way to third in 1959, but traded for outfielder Roger Maris and won the pennant in 1960, the World Series in 1961 and 1962, and pennants in 1963 and 1964. In 1961, Maris hit a record-breaking 61 home runs, and Mantle, batting right behind him, hit 54 more. Not since Babe Ruth and Lou Gehrig had two players and one team so dominated the game.

EDDIE GAEDEL GOES TO BAT

Other teams weren't quite so successful. The cellar-dwelling 1951 St. Louis Browns (52–102) were so desperate for attention that they hired Eddie Gaedel, a 3′7″, 65-pound circus midget, to pinch hit for the leadoff hitter one game. Bill Veeck, the Browns owner, threatened to shoot him if he swung the bat. The scorecard listed him: Number 1/8, Gaedel. Crouched over, his strike zone was 1½ inches high—the width of a matchbook cover. Bobby Cain, the Detroit pitcher, studied him carefully, and fired four pitches over his head. Gaedel trotted to first base, was replaced by a pinch runner, and exited to wild cheers—a perfect career. Within two days, the rules were changed to ban special players like Gaedel from the game.

No one could pitch to the 3′7″ Eddie Gaedel.

Mickey Mantle helped the Yankees stay on top.

THE CUBS COLLEGE OF COACHES

Then there were the Cubs. The poor, sad Chicago Cubs. In 1961, after 14 straight finishes in the bottom half of the standings, owner P.K. Wrigley finally blew his top. Managers don't seem to do us any good, he said, throwing up his hands. And with that he fired manager Lou Boudreau and appointed a "college of coaches."

Every few weeks, for the next two years, the Cubs coaches played musical chairs. The third base coach became the first base coach. The first base coach became the temporary manager. And the previous manager moved back to the third base coaching box. Four "professors"—Vedie Himsl, Harry Craft, Lou Klein and Elvin Tappe—taught the Cubs in 1961, and led the team to a 64–90, seventh-place finish. The next year, Tappe and Klein were joined by a new instructor, Charlie Metro. The Cubs finished even worse, with a 59–103 record.

In 1966, Wrigley hired Leo Durocher to run the team. When reporters asked if he, too, was a coach, the Lip snapped, "I'm not the coach! I'm the *#$%^& manager!" A year later, the club started winning.

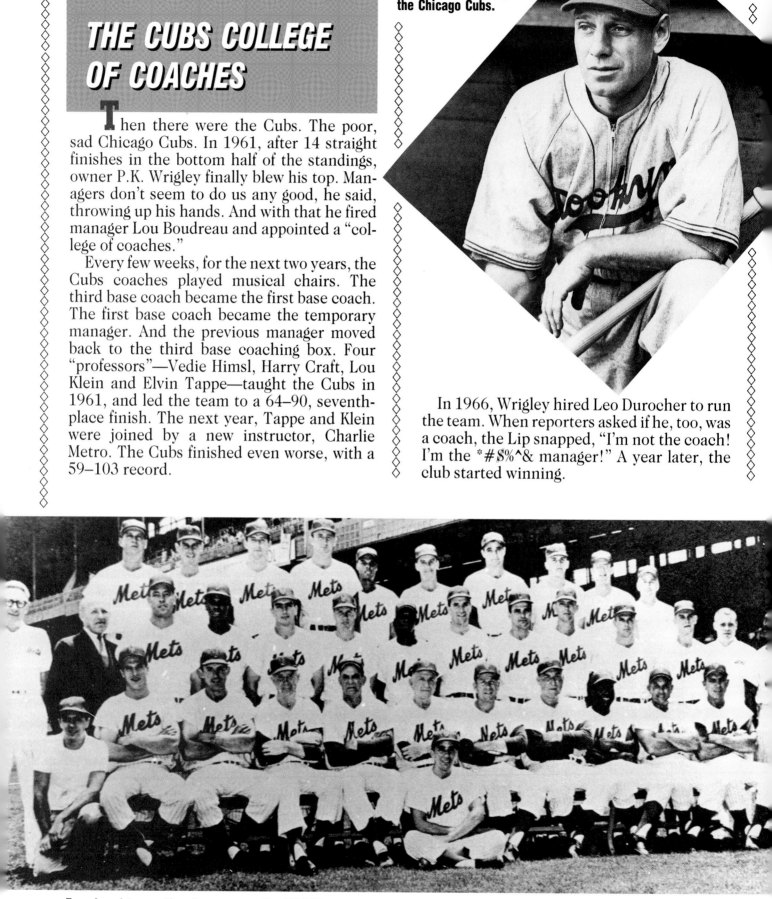

Fans loved to see the strange ways the 1962 Mets would lose.

THE ORIGINAL METS

But even the Cubs never approached the level of losing pioneered by the original New York Mets. Where to begin? Their first year, 1962, they lost 120 games and won just 40. No team had ever been so awful. Fans flocked to see them. People watched them in wonder, to see the bizarre ways they managed to lose.

The Mets that season finished 60½ games out of first place. They had some slight problems with their pitching and defense: The team earned run average was 5.04. (The earned run average, or ERA, is the average number of earned runs scored against a pitcher every nine innings. An ERA under 3.00 is considered good.) Roger Craig, the staff ace, lost 24 games. Al Jackson, the team's second-best pitcher, lost 20. Craig Anderson, the Mets top reliever, went 3–17, with four saves. Rod Kanehl, their late-inning defensive specialist, made 32 errors. In his three-year major league career, Kanehl had more errors

(50) than runs batted in (47). (A batter is credited with a run batted in, or RBI, whenever he causes a runner on base to score by making a hit, sacrifice, infield out, base on balls or by being hit by a pitch.)

In 1963, the Mets improved to only 111 losses. That season, they showcased their hitting. Their starting shortstop, the immortal Al Moran, batted .193. Their starting catcher, Clarence "Choo Choo" Coleman, batted .178, with nine RBIs. Only two regulars batted over .250, and none was as high as .275. The club RBI leader was leftfielder Frank Thomas, who had 60. As a team, the Mets stole 41 bases and batted .219.

A subway ride away from the Mets were the Yankees, the greatest team in the history of the game. But fans seemed to love the Mets best. In their third season, this awful team drew more fans than their pinstriped, crosstown rivals. The greatest thinkers of the day pondered why the world had turned upside down. Yogi Berra, who would later manage the Mets, supplied the answer: "In baseball," he said, "you don't know nothin'."

CHAPTER 2

THE MODERN YEARS

THE MIRACLE METS

Let's take a test. The most incredible event of 1969 was:

A. The United States lands a man on the moon.

B. The Woodstock rock 'n' roll festival.

C. The Mets win the World Series.

If you answered C, you are a true baseball fan. The Mets and winning—you might as well have said peanut butter and mustard—the words didn't seem to go together in the 1960s. This was an amazing change. This was the beginning of the modern baseball era.

The 1969 team was known as the Miracle Mets because in a single year, they leaped

Euphoria after the "Miracle" Mets jumped from ninth place to first in 1969.

Tom Seaver, pitcher for the Mets.

from ninth place and a 73–89 mark to first place and a 100–62 record. It's easy to look back now and see how it happened—their young players all matured at once. But in early 1969, no one knew how good pitchers Tom Seaver, Nolan Ryan, Tug McGraw and Jerry Koosman would become. It seemed as if the team came out of nowhere. The laughingstock of the league turned into a powerhouse overnight. That year, in the World Series, they beat a strong Baltimore Orioles club featuring pitching great Jim Palmer and Hall of Famers Frank Robinson and Brooks Robinson, four games to one. They were a fairy tale come to

life: Like Cinderella, they went from cleaning up after everyone to being the star of the party.

THE RULES CHANGE AND THE PITCHERS TAKE OVER

Almost as important, the Mets captured the imaginations of fans across the country—

New York Yankees Ron Blomberg, the first designated hitter.

HISTORY

fans that had grown bored with the game and had turned instead to football. In the mid-1960s, rule makers had enlarged the strike zone, offsetting the delicate balance between hitting and pitching. In 1968, there was *no* hitting. Pitchers, armed with this huge advantage, threw 339 shutouts. St. Louis pitcher Bob Gibson won the National League ERA championship with a mark of 1.12.

How bad was the mismatch? Boston outfielder Carl Yastrzemski batted .301 and won the American League batting title. The second-best hitter in the league batted .290, and only two others reached .285. The average American League *team* ERA was 2.98; in the National League, it was 2.99. The average American Leaguer batted just .230. The games were low-scoring and boring. Some fans stopped coming to the parks, which caused the owners to worry. Baseball's rules committee shrank the strike zone again and lowered the pitching mound from 15 to 10 inches. In 1969, the revived hitting and the Miracle Mets lured fans back to the game.

THE DH AND THE SAVE RULE

But the owners—at least the American League owners—were still not satisfied. If runs were what the fans wanted, runs were what they would get. In 1973, the American League adopted the designated hitter—the first major rule change since the spitball was outlawed in 1920. It is also the only baseball rule that doesn't apply to both leagues. The National League has repeatedly rejected its use.

In 1973, the save was also added as an official statistic. A relief pitcher is credited with a save if he comes into a game with his team ahead, finishes the game and preserves the win but is not the winning pitcher. (There are also restrictions about how many innings he must pitch depending on what the score is.) The statistic was invented by *Chicago Tribune* baseball columnist Jerome Holtzman to reflect the increasing importance of late-inning relievers. For years, starting pitchers and their managers considered it almost un-

Yankees manager Casey Stengel.

manly not to complete a ball game. Relievers were seen as pitchers who lacked the talent to start.

The first manager to assign a star to the bullpen was Casey Stengel. In 1949 the Yankees manager used fireballer Joe Page in 60 games, and Page responded with 13 wins and a record 27 saves. By contrast, the National League leader that season had just nine saves. The following year, 1950, Phillies reliever Jim Konstanty collected 22 saves, 16 wins and the Most Valuable Player Award. In 1986, the Yankees Dave Righetti set a new record for saves with 46.

Today, top relievers like Righetti, the Cubs Mitch Williams and Dennis Eckersley of the A's are among the biggest stars in the game. They are also among the richest.

BALLPLAYERS BECOME BUSINESSMEN

"Rich" today is a lot different from what "rich" used to be. An average player near the turn of the century made perhaps $3,000 a year. In 1930, when Babe Ruth signed a contract for $80,000, after leading the league in home runs for 10 of the previous 12 years, the nation was shocked. When asked how he could be paid a higher salary than the President of the United States, Ruth replied, "Why not? I had a better year than he did." In 1949, the legendary Yankees centerfielder Joe DiMaggio became the first player to earn $100,000 in a year. Today, the *minimum* major league salary is $100,000, and the average player earns more than $500,000. More than 20 players make over $2 million a year, and in 1993 San Francisco first baseman Will Clark will earn $4 million.

THE FIRST PLAYER STRIKE

These days, it's almost impossible to talk about money without also talking about owner lockouts, arbitration, free agency and player strikes.

It's hard to believe now, but until the late 1960s, very few players had agents to negotiate their contracts. Why? Because the owners wouldn't allow players to have agents. There was a players' union then, but it wasn't very powerful. Player contracts were designed to benefit the owners, not the ballplayers.

In 1972, the players staged a 13-day strike near the end of spring training that canceled 86 games of the regular season. The players returned to the field after the owners agreed to increase the retirement pensions for players.

The players were set to strike again in 1973, when at the last instant the owners granted them the right to arbitration. Arbitration is a process in which a player and his team each submit a salary figure to an impartial judge, who decides which figure seems fairer. This proved to be a great victory for the players. In 1975, an arbitrator awarded players the right to free agency as well. Free agency is a player's right, after playing in the big leagues for a certain number of years, to leave his team and sign with the highest bidder.

By 1976, players such as outfielder Reggie Jackson and Hall of Fame pitcher Catfish

Hunter had changed teams, using free agency to get bigger contracts. The owners, forever crying that they were going broke, somehow managed to find the money to sign top players away from the other teams.

The issue of free agency, however, was still not settled. When the owners tried to limit free agency in 1981, the players went on strike—this time in the middle of the season. They stopped playing on June 12 and didn't return until August 1, 50 days later. It was the longest strike in the history of the sport.

The most recent labor strife occurred in 1990, when for the second time (the first was in 1976) the owners locked the players out of spring training camps. Once again, the issue was arbitration. But the two sides reached a settlement near the end of spring training, allowing the regular season to start one week late.

Wait a minute—is this a sports book or a business book? Can we get back to baseball?

CHARLIE FINLEY'S A'S

The greatest team of the modern era had a mule as its mascot, had players who

Club owner Charlie Finley built the A's into a winning team.

fought each other in the clubhouse, and had a wacky, cantankerous owner who paid his players to grow mustaches. Meet the Oakland A's of the early 1970s. They were as wild as the Cardinals' 1934 Gashouse Gang, and they played even better.

They won five straight American League West titles, and three straight world championships. Their stars included Reggie Jackson and Catfish Hunter, 20-game winners Ken Holtzman and Vida Blue, speedy Billy North, and shortstop Bert "Campy" Campaneris, the Ozzie Smith of his time.

Club owner Charlie Finley was a genius at some things. He was a millionaire who made his fortune in the insurance business. He quickly developed a keen eye for baseball talent, and he traded for and discovered many of the A's biggest stars. He was also a wonderful promoter. Holding the World Series and All-Star games at night was his idea. Unfortunately for the A's, he could also be harsh and uncaring. When second baseman Mike Andrews made two errors during the 1973 World Series, Finley tried to remove him from the team.

After winning that Series, manager Dick Williams announced that he had had enough of Finley's meddling, and quit. Almost as soon as free agency was created, many of his players—among them Jackson, Hunter and team captain Sal Bando—left, just as Williams had. The A's quickly sank to the bottom of the division, where they remained until 1980. Finley sold the team in 1981.

BILLY AND GEORGE AND THE YANKEES

But life in Oakland was a picnic compared to the George Steinbrenner years with the New York Yankees. From 1973, when he

Billy Martin, the argumentative manager of the Yankees.

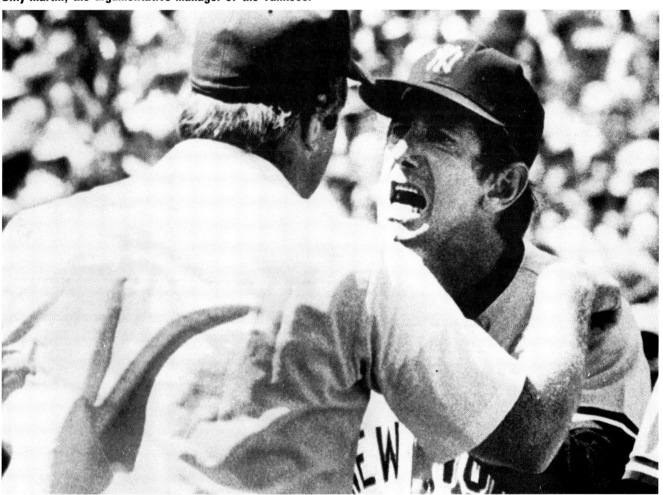

took control of the team, until 1990, he changed managers 18 times. He hired and fired Billy Martin five times. He hired and fired Bob Lemon, Gene Michael and Lou Piniella twice. Several of his greatest players—including Reggie Jackson and ace reliever Goose Gossage—left the Yankees for other teams so they wouldn't have to work for him. Sparky Lyle, a former Yankees reliever, titled his autobiography, appropriately, *The Bronx Zoo.*

Still, the Yankees did manage to win four pennants and two World Series in those years, often with Billy Martin managing. The belligerent, feisty manager was just as tough as Steinbrenner, and the two were often at each other's throats. Steinbrenner never seemed to

agree with Martin as to how the team should be managed, but he kept rehiring him. Whether it's because of all the managerial changes or in spite of them, one thing is sure: The once mighty Yankees dynasty isn't what it used to be.

THE FALL OF PETE ROSE

Despite all the noise, all the business and politics, it looked as if there was at least one player left who was completely devoted to

Pete Rose, one of the all-time great batters.

baseball. That was Pete Rose. In 1978, he hit in 44 straight games—the longest batting streak since DiMaggio's 56-game streak in 1941. Rose was 37 during the streak, and still played with the boyish enthusiasm of an 11-year-old. He dove headfirst into bases. He ran out everything, even bases on balls. When Rose got home at night, he turned on the TV and watched baseball until he fell asleep. All he thought about was hitting baseballs.

On September 11, 1985, Rose lined a single to left center off San Diego pitcher Eric Show—his 4,192nd major league hit. Rose had finally broken Ty Cobb's record. He retired the next season with a record 4,256 career hits, a seemingly unbeatable mark. Rose played in more games than anyone in history. He played in more *winning* games than any other player. He ranks first all-time in hits and at bats, second in doubles, fourth in runs scored and sixth in total bases. Wheaties put his face on its boxes.

But even Rose proved less than perfect. In 1989, a scandal broke that ended Rose's fantastic career. He was banned from baseball for life for betting on sports events. He was forced to resign as manager of the Cincinnati Reds, the team for which he had played most of his career. It looked to some fans like the Black Sox scandal all over again. Once again, gambling had darkened the national pastime.

But baseball is bigger than any one player, any labor contract, any club owner. The beauty of the game, the thrill of a great performance can make us forget the other stuff. Sometimes, all it takes is one crack of the bat or one spectacular catch. And as we enter the 1990s, it's not gambling or free agency that we think about—it's the game and the players. Can Jose Canseco, Mark McGwire, Dennis Eckersley and Dave Stewart lead the Oakland A's to more championships? Will Ken Griffey Jr., Alvin Davis and Harold Reynolds lead the Mariners to their first winning season in history? Will Bo Jackson hit 50 homers for the Royals? Will George Brett get 3,000 hits? Will Bret Saberhagen win a third Cy Young Award?

It's baseball, man. It's baseball.

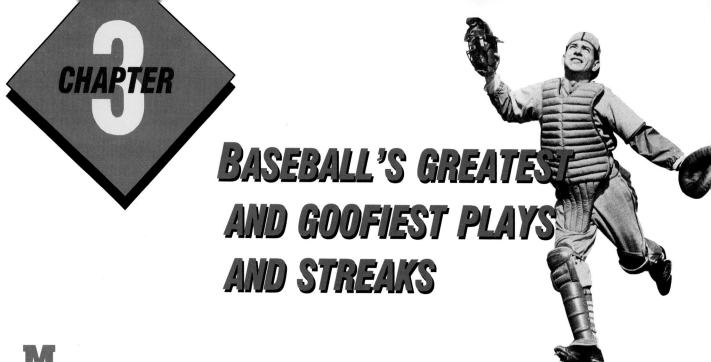

CHAPTER 3

BASEBALL'S GREATEST AND GOOFIEST PLAYS AND STREAKS

Most serious baseball fans are closet accountants. Throw out any name—Hack Wilson, who starred for the Cubs in the early 1930s, or Shoeless Joe Jackson, who played for the White Sox from 1916 to 1920—and the true fan will toss back a mess of statistics (batting averages, stolen base totals, slugging percentages, etc.) It doesn't matter that Wilson played 60 years ago and Jackson played 75 years ago because numbers are how we stay connected to the game. They give us a sense of history.

But the memories we take from the game aren't cold numbers. What we remember are the plays—the ones that inspired us, the ones that won or lost championships, the ones that made us laugh or cheer. We may not have seen the plays in person. After all, there are only so many thousands of fans that can fit into a ballpark. But we've heard the stories, seen the pictures or watched the game on TV. And we can imagine what it was like.

The *numbers* say that Mickey Mantle hit 536 career home runs, but what we remember is the 565-foot homer he blasted in Griffith Stadium against the Washington Senators in 1953.

The numbers say that former Cubs first baseman Joe Pepitone sat on the bench for quite a few ball games, but what we remember is that once Pepitone refused to leave the dugout after his hairpiece had slipped off near home plate.

If the Hall of Fame could close its eyes, it wouldn't see numbers, either. It would see plays and performances such as these:

1908 "BONEHEAD" MERKLE'S BONEHEAD PLAY

The New York Giants and the Chicago Cubs were tied in the standings when the two teams met September 23, 1908, at the Polo Grounds in New York. The score was tied, 1–1, in the bottom of the ninth. There were two outs. Giants outfielder "Moose" McCormick was on third base and 19-year-old rookie first baseman Fred Merkle was on first. Shortstop Al Bridwell lined a single over second base and into right centerfield. McCormick loped home to score the apparent winning run.

But the run didn't count. Merkle turned around and headed for the dugout without bothering to touch second. Cubs second baseman Johnny Evers called for the ball and touched the base. Merkle was forced out.

Meanwhile, thousands of spectators had poured onto the field, thinking the Giants had

"Bonehead" Merkle earned his name when he lost the Giants their pennant.

won. The game was played over on October 8, with the two teams tied for first. This time, the Cubs won, 4–2, and captured the pennant. Afterwards, Giants fans changed Merkle's first name from Fred to "Bonehead."

1926 BABE HERMAN TRIPLES INTO A DOUBLE PLAY

The 1926 Brooklyn Dodgers were known as "The Daffiness Boys," because they played like Charlie Brown's team. They loaded the bases one afternoon against the seventh-place Boston Braves. Floyd "Babe" Herman, their hard-hitting but soft-thinking rookie first baseman, came to bat. With one out in the seventh inning and the score tied, 1–1, Herman boomed a towering shot to right center.

The runners weren't sure if the ball would be caught, so they stayed near their bases. Herman just put his head down and ran. The ball hit the fence and the runner on third trotted home. Pitcher Dazzy Vance, who ran slower than thick catsup, lumbered from second around third and headed for the plate. The ball was relayed back toward the infield.

A problem arose. Second baseman Chick Fewster was sprinting from first around the bases toward third. Right behind him was Herman. "Back! Back!" screamed the Dodg-

Floyd "Babe" Herman, one of the "Daffiness Boys."

ers third base coach. His shouts were meant for Herman, but Vance was the one who responded. He braked midway to the plate and dove back to third. Fewster dove, too. So did Herman. When the dust cleared, all three stood on third base.

Unfortunately, Vance was the only one entitled to be there. Herman was immediately tagged out, but somehow the Braves third baseman missed Fewster. Boston's second baseman chased Fewster into rightfield and finally tagged him with the ball on top of his head. "He shoulda tagged him with a blackjack," snapped Dodgers manager Wilbert Robinson afterwards.

1932 BABE RUTH'S CALLED SHOT

Some of this is absolutely true, some of it may be pure legend. Here is what we know: The Babe was near the end of his career when the Yankees faced the Chicago Cubs in the 1932 World Series. In the first two games, both won by the Yankees, the Cubs taunted Ruth mercilessly.

Charlie Root started Game 3 for the Cubs, before 50,000 fans at Wrigley Field. The Babe blasted a three-run homer in the first inning. When he came up again in the fifth, the razzing grew even louder. Ruth stepped to the plate and took a called strike. The Cubs players screamed at him. Ruth looked over to the Chicago dugout and grinned. He raised one finger of his right hand, as if to say, "That's one." Root threw two balls, and then another called strike. With the Cubs and their fans hooting at him, Ruth raised two fingers.

What happened next is unclear. Legend has it that Ruth pointed to the centerfield bleachers with his finger. Gabby Hartnett, the Cubs catcher, swears he heard him say, "It only takes one to hit it." Lou Gehrig, in the on-deck circle, says he heard Ruth yell to Root, "I'm going to knock the next pitch right down your throat."

The Cubs pitcher threw a slow curve, low and away. Ruth clubbed it on a line into the centerfield bleachers, right to the place where some say he had just pointed. Could even the great Babe do that? Did he point to where he planned to hit it? Ruth would never say.

1941 JOE DIMAGGIO'S 56-GAME HITTING STREAK

You can never say never, but this record seems as unapproachable as any. In the summer of 1941, the whole nation seemed caught up in DiMaggio's streak.

When it began, on May 15, many thought DiMaggio was on his way to an untypically poor season. He had batted .194 over the previous 20 games. His only hit that day was a harmless single.

The newspapers began following the streak

Yankees Joe DiMaggio still holds the record for the longest batting streak.

in earnest when DiMaggio reached 18 games on June 1. In fact, they were following two streaks. For 23 games, Ted Williams matched DiMaggio game for game. Williams batted an incredible .489 over those games, while DiMaggio batted .374. Then Williams went hitless, and the nation completely focused on DiMaggio.

He nearly lost his streak June 1, when Cleveland third baseman Ken Keltner made a marvelous stop of a smash down the third base line, but couldn't throw DiMaggio out. He seemed in trouble again in Game 45, the one that would break Wee Willie Keeler's all-time record. Boston rightfielder Sam Spence sprinted deep into right center and made a circus catch of DiMaggio's long fly in the first inning. Later in the game, however, the Yankee Clipper homered and set a new record.

On July 16, he hit in his 56th straight game. The next day, against the Indians in Cleveland, DiMaggio hit two terrific smashes to Keltner in his first and third at bats, each for outs. Starting pitcher Al Smith walked him in his second at bat, bringing a chorus of boos from the Cleveland crowd. In his final at bat, in the eighth inning against reliever Jim Bagby, he grounded to Lou Boudreau at short.

The following day, DiMaggio began a new,

16-game hitting streak. He went on to win the Most Valuable Player award that season, batting .357, with 30 homers and a league-leading 125 RBIs. As for Williams, he never cooled off. The Boston slugger hit .406 that year. No one has hit .400 since. It was quite a summer for baseball.

1941 MICKEY OWEN'S DROPPED THIRD STRIKE

Mickey Owen was an average catcher who in 1941 was lucky enough to be on Brooklyn's first pennant winner in 21 years. He was catching in the ninth inning of Game 4 of the World Series, with the Dodgers ahead, 4–3, and about to tie the Series at two games apiece.

With two out, nobody on and two strikes on, Yankee first baseman Tommy Henrich, Dodgers relief pitcher Hugh Casey threw a hard sinker on the outside corner. Henrich swung

Mickey Owens, the Dodgers catcher who missed the pitch.

and missed, and the umpire called, "Strike three!" Unfortunately, Owen missed the pitch, too. It bounced off his glove and rolled toward the backstop. Henrich reached first, and the Yankees rallied to win the game. They won the next day, too, to win the World Series, four games to one.

1951 BOBBY THOMSON'S "SHOT HEARD 'ROUND THE WORLD"

On July 27, 1951, the New York Giants were half a game out of last place. In mid-August, they still trailed the league-leading Brooklyn Dodgers by 13½ games. But, with an

Bobby Thomson's "shot heard 'round the world."

incredible rush, they tied the Dodgers at the end of the regular season and forced a three-game playoff for the pennant. The Giants won the first game; the Dodgers took the second. Brooklyn was poised to win the third game and the pennant as it took a 4–1 lead into the bottom of the ninth at the Polo Grounds.

But then Don Newcombe, the Dodgers ace pitcher, began to tire. The first two Giants hitters singled. With one out, Giants first baseman Whitey Lockman doubled, scoring one run and putting men on second and third. The Dodgers had two pitchers warming up in the bullpen, starter Ralph Branca and rookie reliever Clem Labine. The bullpen coach signaled that Labine was bouncing his curve. Manager Charlie Dressen chose Branca.

Third baseman Bobby Thomson, who had hit 31 home runs already that year, stepped to the plate. He let the first pitch go by for a strike. Then he clubbed the second one into the leftfield seats. With that one home run, the Giants won the playoff and the pennant. It was the most dramatic home run in baseball history.

1954 WILLIE MAYS'S WORLD SERIES CATCH

Willie Mays returned from Army duty in 1954 and batted .345, hit 41 homers and knocked in 110 runs to win the MVP Award and lead the New York Giants to the World Series against the Cleveland Indians.

Game 1 was played at the spacious Polo Grounds. The score was tied, 2–2, in the top of the eighth inning when the Indians put runners on first and second with nobody out. Vic Wertz, a slugging Cleveland outfielder, clubbed a 440-foot drive over Mays's head in dead center. No one but Mays could have made the play. He made a spectacular over-the-shoulder catch, and then in one motion, pivoted and fired the ball back to the infield.

Willie Mays's incredible over-the-shoulder catch.

The Indians didn't score. The Giants went on to win the game in the 10th inning, and swept the Tribe four games to none.

1956 DON LARSEN'S PERFECT GAME

Don Larsen, when all is said and done, was an average pitcher at best. He had a career record of 81–91, with a 3.78 ERA, and in 14 years pitched for eight different teams. In his second big league season, pitching for the Orioles, Larsen went 3–21. For four years, he walked more men than he struck out. Yet on October 8, 1956, he pitched the only perfect game in World Series history.

Larsen was with the Yankees that year, and they were facing the Dodgers in the Series. Three days earlier, Brooklyn had knocked him out of Game 2 in just 1⅔ innings. Now, entering Game 5, the teams were tied with two wins apiece.

As Larsen pitched, his previous record didn't seem to matter. Using his no-windup delivery, he was both lucky and invincible. No one had ever pitched a no-hitter in the Series, but inning after improbable inning Larsen retired every batter he faced.

The Dodgers hit some terrific shots, but the Yankees played beautiful defense. With each play, the perfect game hung in the balance. Centerfielder Mickey Mantle made an over-the-shoulder catch of first baseman Gil Hodges's 430-foot drive to centerfield. Jackie

Robinson hit a smash off third baseman Andy Carey's glove that caromed to shortstop Gil McDougald, who threw Robinson out at first.

With two out in the ninth, the Dodgers sent Dale Mitchell up to pinch hit. One strike came, then another. When Mitchell was called out, looking at a strike on the outside corner of the plate, the crowd and the Yankees went absolutely wild. Larsen had thrown 97 pitches to get 27 outs. He had not allowed a single hit or base on balls. He won his perfect game, 2–0, and two days later the Yankees won the World Series.

1974 HANK AARON'S 715TH HOME RUN

Hank Aaron ended the 1973 season with 713 home runs. He had the entire winter to think about breaking Babe Ruth's career

Don Larsen, the only pitcher to throw a perfect World Series game.

Hank Aaron hitting his 715th home run.

home run record of 714. What he wanted, most of all, was to get it over with quickly. There were more reporters following Aaron than were following the President of the United States.

He hit number 714 with his very first swing of the 1974 season. He tagged that home run off Cincinnati pitcher Jack Billingham on opening day, in the first inning. With two men on and one out and a 3–1 count on Aaron, Billingham threw a fastball over the heart of the plate. Aaron turned on it, and lined it over the left centerfield fence. Now the record was tied. One more home run would break it.

He hit the record breaker four days later, on April 8, in Atlanta's home opener against the Dodgers. Dodgers starter Al Downing walked Aaron on five pitches in the second inning. Aaron never swung the bat. Two innings later he came up again, this time with a man on base. Downing's first pitch was a changeup inside. His second was a fastball that stayed high over the plate. With his first swing of the game, Aaron lofted the ball over the left centerfield fence into the Braves bullpen. The crowd became hysterical. This was the moment that everyone, including Aaron himself, had been waiting for. The chase was over. Aaron had done what some people had said was impossible—he had beaten the Babe!

Aaron played the rest of the season with the Braves, hitting 18 more homers. In November, he was traded to the Milwaukee Brewers. He played two more seasons before retiring in 1976 with a record 755 career home runs.

1977 REGGIE JACKSON'S FIVE WORLD SERIES HOME RUNS

Babe Ruth hit four World Series homers in 1926. Lou Gehrig matched him in 1928. Duke Snider hit four twice, in 1952 and 1955. Oakland catcher Gene Tenace hit four in 1972, and so did Yankee outfielder Hank Bauer in 1958.

No one had hit five in a single series. No one, that is, until Reggie Jackson went on his incredible tear in 1977. For the Yankee right-fielder, it was a storybook ending to a very troubled year.

He had joined the Yankees that spring, after signing a big-bucks free agent contract. When a magazine reporter asked about his role on the team, Reggie arrogantly replied, "I'm the straw that stirs the drink." Several of his teammates openly resented him. He spent the summer at odds with his manager, Billy Martin.

But he hit a home run in Game 4 of the World Series against the Dodgers and helped put the Yankees ahead, three games to one. He hit another homer a day later in a Yankees loss. Then, in the sixth and final game of the Series, he really went to work. He hit three successive homers, each on the first pitch, to carry the Yankees to victory.

He became the most famous athlete in America. He became known as Mr. October for his outstanding postseason performance. Someone even named a candy bar—the Reggie Bar—after him.

1988 OREL HERSHISER'S 59-INNING SHUTOUT STREAK

Orel Hershiser was having a fantastic year even before he began his shutout streak late in the 1988 season. He tossed the fifth two-hitter of his career on June 29 at Houston, lifting his record to 12–3. Then he kicked into high gear.

Hershiser threw two consecutive complete games before the streak, which began August 30 with four shutout innings to end a game against the Montreal Expos. Then he threw five successive shutouts against the Atlanta Braves (twice), the Cincinnati Reds,

Reggie Jackson hit five home runs in one World Series.

the Houston Astros and the San Francisco Giants.

Hall of Famer Don Drysdale, a former Dodger, had thrown 58 straight shutout innings in 1968 to set the major league record. Hershisher was still nine innings short of Drysdale's mark and he had just one scheduled start left in the season. His only chance to break the record was to pitch a 10-inning shutout while his own team was being blanked.

Fortunately for Hershiser, the 1988 Dodgers were a team of hitless wonders. They finished tied for sixth in total runs, and batted only .248. On September 28, against San Diego, his teammates "came through" for Orel. Hershiser pitched 10 scoreless innings in a game the Dodgers would eventually lose in 16 innings. Unofficially, he extended the streak to 67 innings during the playoffs against the Mets.

During those 59 regular season innings, he allowed just 31 hits and gave up 11 walks. He struck out 38. By the end of the streak, he had thrown eight straight complete games. He ended the year 23–8, with two complete game victories over Oakland in the World Series. He won the Cy Young Award.

Dodgers Orel Hershiser threw an amazing 59-inning shutout.

CHAPTER 4

TIME LINE

1845 On October 21, the earliest known report of a baseball game is published in the *New York Morning News*.

1869 Harry Wright forms the Cincinnati Red Stockings, the first professional baseball team. The Red Stockings go 56–0–1, and the team earns a net profit of $1.39.

1871 On March 17, nine club owners meet in New York to form the National Association of Professional Base Ball Players, baseball's first professional league.

1875 Repeated gambling and bribery charges cause the public to lose confidence in the National Association. The league folds at the end of the season.

1876 William A. Hulbert, a Chicago businessman, spearheads the formation of a new professional baseball league, the National League. The Boston Red Caps and Philadelphia Athletics play the league's first game on April 22, with Boston winning, 6–5.

1882 Six new clubs form a rival professional league, the American Association. The two leagues compete with each other for players. For a time, the American Association outdraws the National League because it is willing to schedule Sunday games, but it folds after the 1891 season.

1884 Catcher Fleet Walker and his brother, outfielder Welday Walker, play for To-

ledo of the American Association. They are the only blacks to play in the major leagues until Jackie Robinson joins the Brooklyn Dodgers in 1947.

1885 The Brotherhood of Professional Ball Players, baseball's first players' union, is formed. The union's main concerns are low salaries and the reserve clause in players' contracts. (Sound familiar?)

1894 Boston outfielder Hugh Duffy bats .438.

1894 Louisville third baseman Jerry Denny, the last player to play without a glove, retires.

1897 Baltimore outfielder Wee Willie Keeler hits safely in 44 consecutive games.

Baltimore outfielder Wee Willie Keeler.

Chicago's double play combination Tinker, Evers and Chance.

1897 The Chicago Colts of the National League score 36 runs in a nine-inning game.

1901 Ex-sportswriter Ban Johnson forms the American League and lures away many of the National League's top stars.

1903 The most famous double play combination in history—Joe Tinker, Johnny Evers and Frank Chance—play together regularly for the Chicago Cubs for the first of many seasons. They are immortalized in a poem by Franklin P. Adams, though they are an average double play combo at best. All three eventually make the Hall of Fame.

1903 The Boston Red Sox beat the Pittsburgh Pirates in the first World Series.

1904 New York Giants manager John McGraw refuses to play the American League champions in the World Series, so the games are canceled.

1905 The New York Giants beat the Philadelphia Athletics four games to one in the World Series. All five games are shutouts.

1911 Cy Young retires after winning 511 games. He loses his final game, 1–0, at the age of 44.

1912 New York Giants pitcher Rube Marquard wins 19 consecutive games.

1913 Walter Johnson pitches 55⅔ consecutive scoreless innings for the Washington Senators. New York Giants pitcher Christy Mathewson pitches 68 consecutive innings without permitting a walk.

1914 A group of businessmen forms the Federal League and raids the National and American Leagues for players. The Fed-

The Washington Senators pitcher, Walter Johnson.

eral League folds after the 1915 season.

1916 The New York Giants play 26 consecutive games without a loss. (The streak does include one tie.)

1917 Cincinnati Reds pitcher Fred Toney and Chicago Cubs pitcher James "Hippo" Vaughn pitch baseball's only double no-hitter. Toney pitches a no-hitter for 10 innings, to beat Vaughn, who pitched a no-hitter for 9⅓ innings.

1919 Ty Cobb bats .384 to win his 12th batting championship in 13 years. In 1916, he had finished second with a .371 average.

1919 The New York Giants beat the Philadelphia Phillies, 6–1, in 51 minutes, the quickest major league game in history.

1919 For $100,000, eight Chicago White Sox agree to throw the World Series to the underdog Cincinnati Reds. A year later, the eight are expelled from baseball for life.

1920 Baseball introduces the "lively" ball, which goes farther when hit. Babe Ruth hits 54 home runs, almost doubling the major league record of 29 he had hit in 1919. In 1921, he hits 59.

1920 The spitball is declared illegal.

1920 Cleveland Indians second baseman Bill Wambsganss completes the only unassisted triple play in World Series history against the Brooklyn Dodgers.

1922 On August 25, the Chicago Cubs beat the Philadelphia Phillies, 26–23, in the highest scoring game in major league history.

1925 St. Louis Cardinals second baseman Rogers Hornsby bats .403, the third time in four years he has topped the .400 mark. In 1924 he had batted .424.

St. Louis Cardinals Rogers Hornsby.

1927 Babe Ruth hits 60 home runs.

1931 St. Louis Cardinals second baseman Frankie Frisch (who had a .311 batting average) and Philadelphia Athletics pitcher Lefty Grove (who had a 31–4 won-lost record) win the first Most Valuable Player Awards.

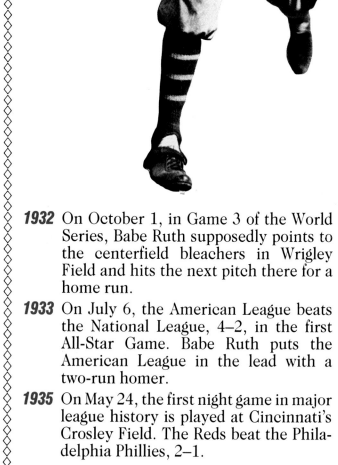

Cardinals Frankie Frisch and Athletics Lefty Grove win the first Most Valuable Player Awards.

1932 On October 1, in Game 3 of the World Series, Babe Ruth supposedly points to the centerfield bleachers in Wrigley Field and hits the next pitch there for a home run.

1933 On July 6, the American League beats the National League, 4–2, in the first All-Star Game. Babe Ruth puts the American League in the lead with a two-run homer.

1935 On May 24, the first night game in major league history is played at Cincinnati's Crosley Field. The Reds beat the Philadelphia Phillies, 2–1.

Tony Lazzeri, one of only six players ever to hit two grand slams in one game.

Johnny Vandermeer, pitcher for the Cincinnati Reds.

Boston Red Sox Ted Williams, the last player to bat over .400 in one season.

1936 On May 24, New York Yankees second baseman Tony Lazzeri hits two grand slams in a single game. Only six other players have equalled his feat.

1938 On June 11, Cincinnati Reds pitcher Johnny Vander Meer throws a no-hitter against the Boston Bees (now the Atlanta Braves). Four days later, during the first night game at Brooklyn's Ebbets Field, he pitches his second straight no-hitter, this time against the Brooklyn Dodgers.

1941 From May 15 to July 16, New York Yankee centerfielder Joe DiMaggio hits safely in 56 consecutive games.

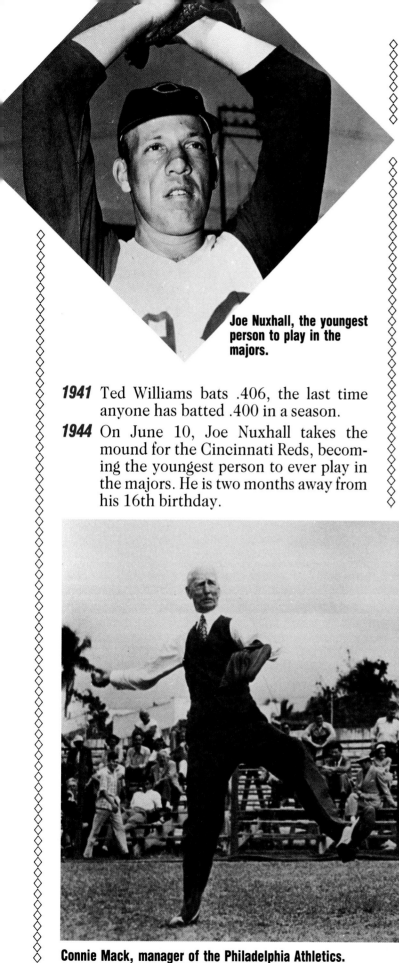

Joe Nuxhall, the youngest person to play in the majors.

1941 Ted Williams bats .406, the last time anyone has batted .400 in a season.

1944 On June 10, Joe Nuxhall takes the mound for the Cincinnati Reds, becoming the youngest person to ever play in the majors. He is two months away from his 16th birthday.

1945 One-armed outfielder Pete Gray bats .218 for the St. Louis Browns and one-legged pitcher Bert Shepard pitches 5⅓ innings of one-run ball for the Washington Senators.

1947 Brooklyn Dodgers first baseman Jackie Robinson becomes the first black player in the major leagues since 1884. He wins the first Rookie of the Year Award, batting .297 and leading the Dodgers to the World Series.

1950 Connie Mack retires after managing the Philadelphia Athletics for 50 years.

1951 Eddie Gaedel, all 43 inches of him, bats leadoff for the St. Louis Browns and is walked on four pitches. His uniform number is 1/8.

1951 New York Giants centerfielder Willie Mays makes a barehanded catch of Pittsburgh Pirates first baseman Rocky Nelson's 457-foot smash to dead center.

1953 Mickey Mantle hits a 565-foot home run off Washington Senators pitcher Chuck Stobbs in Washington's Griffith Stadium. It is still the longest home run ever measured.

Connie Mack, manager of the Philadelphia Athletics.

1953 The New York Yankees defeat the Brooklyn Dodgers to win a record fifth straight World Series.

1955 The Brooklyn Dodgers win their first World Series, beating the New York Yankees four games to three on Johnny Podres's 2–0 seventh-game shutout.

1956 Brooklyn Dodgers pitcher Don Newcombe finishes the season 27–7 and wins the first Cy Young Award.

1956 On October 8, in Game 5 of the World Series, New York Yankees pitcher Don Larsen hurls the only perfect game in Series history. The Yankees beat the Brooklyn Dodgers, 2–0.

1958 The Brooklyn Dodgers and New York Giants leave New York City, the Dodgers resettling in Los Angeles and the Giants in San Francisco.

Don Newcombe, winner of the first Cy Young award.

Roger Maris's 61st home run.

1959 On May 29 against the Milwaukee Braves, Pittsburgh Pirates pitcher Harvey Haddix throws 12 innings of perfect baseball. He loses the game in the 13th inning, when Braves first baseman Joe Adcock slams a home run.

1961 The American League expands to 10 teams.

1961 On October 1, the final day of the season, New York Yankees outfielder Roger Maris blasts a home run into the right-field bleachers off Tracy Stallard of the Boston Red Sox. For Maris, it is his 61st homer of the season and it breaks Babe Ruth's single-season record. Maris takes 162 games to break the record. Ruth had set the record in only 154.

1962 The National League expands to 10 teams. It is the New York Mets first season. They finish 40–120.

1962 The San Francisco Giants catch the Los Angeles Dodgers and finish in a tie for first place. Again. The playoff goes three games. Again. The Dodgers lose in the ninth inning of Game 3. Again.

1963 Late in the season, the San Francisco Giants play Matty Alou in leftfield, his brother Felipe in center and their brother Jesus in right.

1966 The Major League Baseball Players Association, the players' union, is formed.

1969 Both leagues expand to 12 teams. The "amazin'" New York Mets win the National League pennant and then beat the heavily favored Baltimore Orioles, four games to one, in the World Series.

1970 After the St. Louis Cardinals attempt to trade him to the Philadelphia Phillies, outfielder Curt Flood challenges baseball's reserve clause, which restricts a player's freedom to move from team to team. Flood sues major league baseball, but loses.

1972 The players stage their first strike, wiping out the first 10 days of the season.

1973 Nolan Ryan strikes out a record 383 batters.

Frank Robinson, baseball's first black manager.

Fred Lynn, first rookie to win the Most Valuable Player Award.

1973 The American League adopts the designated hitter rule.

1974 On April 8, Hank Aaron hits his 715th home run, breaking Babe Ruth's career record.

1974 Nolan Ryan, then of the California Angels, throws a pitch 100.9 miles per hour.

1974 The Oakland A's win their third consecutive World Series, beating the Los Angeles Dodgers, four games to one.

1975 Frank Robinson becomes baseball's first black manager. He is hired as the Cleveland Indians player-manager.

1975 On September 28, the final day of the season, four Oakland A's pitchers—Vida Blue, Glenn Abbott, Paul Lindblad and Rollie Fingers—combine to pitch a no-hitter against the California Angels. The A's win, 5–0.

1975 Boston Red Sox outfielder Fred Lynn becomes the first rookie ever to win the Most Valuable Player Award.

1975 The Cincinnati Reds beat the Boston Red Sox, four games to three, in what is perhaps the most exciting World Series ever. Boston wins Game 6 when Carlton

Red Sox pitcher Roger Clemens.

Fisk homers in the 12th inning. Cincinnati overcomes a 3–0 Boston lead to take the final game.

1975 An arbitrator strikes down baseball's reserve clause, opening the way for free agency.

1976 Baseball's owners lock the players out of spring training camp for 17 days.

1976 Free agency is adopted by baseball. Twenty-four players opt for free agency. Reggie Jackson signs a five-year, $3 million contract with the New York Yankees.

1976 Hank Aaron retires after hitting a record 755 home runs.

1977 The American League adds two teams.

1977 Yankees outfielder Reggie Jackson hits a record five home runs against the Los Angeles Dodgers in the World Series. He hits three in the final game on three consecutive swings.

1978 Cincinnati Reds outfielder Pete Rose ties a National League mark by hitting in 44 consecutive games.

1981 The players strike for 50 days in mid-season, causing baseball to play a split season.

1981 On September 26, Nolan Ryan (then with the Houston Astros) pitches a record fifth no-hitter, beating the Los Angeles Dodgers, 5–0. He joins Cy Young and Jim Bunning as the only pitchers to have thrown no-hitters in each league.

1982 Oakland A's outfielder Rickey Henderson steals a record 130 bases.

1985 The players walk out on August 6, protesting the lack of a contract between their union and management. They return to the field two days later.

1985 On September 11, Cincinnati Reds player-manager Pete Rose singles to leftfield off San Diego Padres pitcher Eric Show. It is Rose's 4,192nd hit and it breaks Ty Cobb's career record. Rose retires in 1986 with 4,256 hits.

1986 On April 29, Boston Red Sox pitcher Roger Clemens strikes out a record 20 Seattle Mariners in a nine-inning game.

Jose Canseco, baseball's
first 40–40 man.

1988 New York Yankees owner George Steinbrenner hires and fires manager Billy Martin for the fifth and final time.

1988 On August 8, Wrigley Field becomes the final major league ballpark to be lit up. Their first night game is rained out after 3½ innings. The next night, the Chicago Cubs win their first official home night game, 6–4, over the New York Mets.

1988 Oakland A's outfielder Jose Canseco hits 42 home runs and steals 40 bases, and becomes baseball's first 40–40 man.

1988 Los Angeles Dodgers pitcher Orel Hershiser hurls 59 consecutive scoreless innings, breaking Don Drysdale's major league record.

1989 Nolan Ryan, 42 years old and playing for the Texas Rangers, strikes out 301 batters, giving him a record 5,076 for his career. Only one other pitcher has even struck out *4,000* batters.

1989 The Oakland A's beat the San Francisco Giants, four games to none, in a World Series postponed by a terrible earthquake.

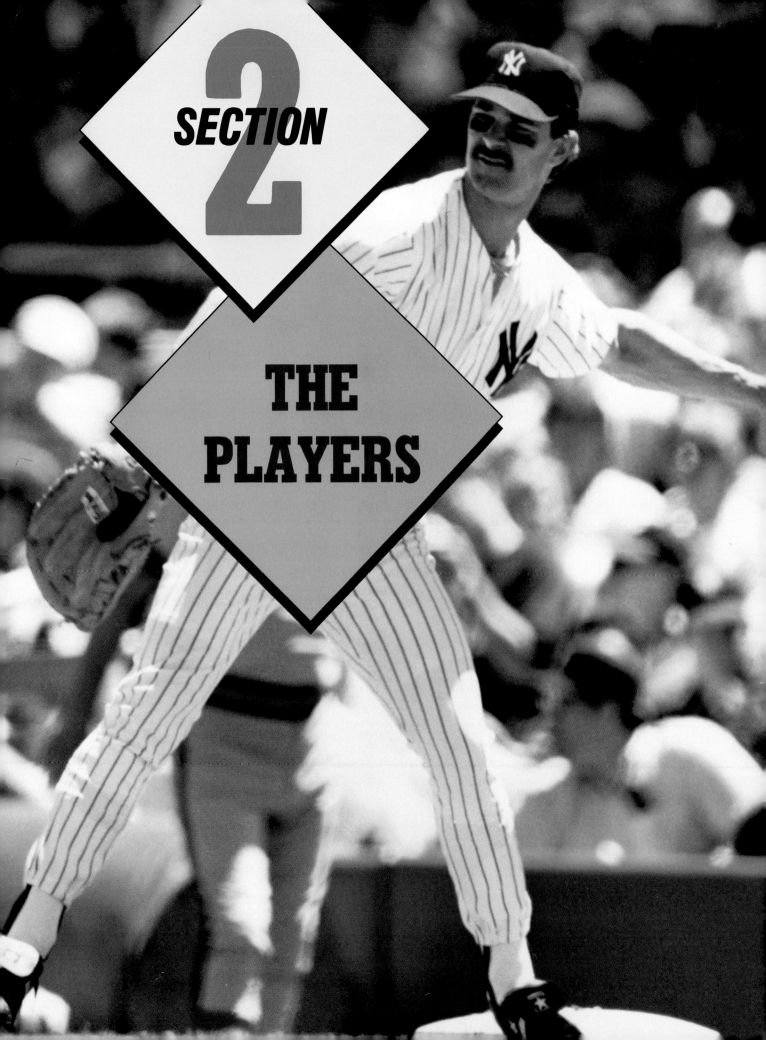

SECTION 2

THE PLAYERS

CHAPTER 5

TODAY'S BIG NAMES

It's easy to say in cold numbers what makes a great ballplayer. For a hitter, it's 40 home runs, 100 RBIs and a .300 batting average. For a pitcher, it's 20 wins or 30 saves, and a microscopic ERA. But it's how they go about reaching those numbers that makes players come alive for us. Rick Reuschel and Dwight Gooden have both been 20-game winners, but their paths to success couldn't be more different. One throws junkballs, the other throws a heater. One is chunky, the other is skinny. One is in his 40s, the other is in his 20s. One is from a farm, the other is from the city. It's watching how their stories unfold that brings out the fan in us. Here are snapshots of some of the best in the game today:

THE BEST OF THE NATIONAL LEAGUE:

Will Clark

"Will the Thrill," Giants fans call him. In fact, it is what he calls himself. Say that he's cocky and he'll probably agree. But he can do almost everything you could ever dream of on a baseball field.

Clark has the prettiest swing in the majors. It's compact and controlled, yet as powerful as a Mike Tyson punch. He never seems off-balance. Most power men are pull hitters, but the lefthanded Clark is skilled at using the entire field. Throw him an outside pitch and he'll smack a double down the leftfield line.

He came to the Giants in 1986, at age 22,

Will Clark, known to his fans as "Will the Thrill."

after batting .429 for the 1984 U.S. Olympic team. The first major league pitch he swung at he hit for a home run. The pitcher who threw that ball was Nolan Ryan. Nice start!

Clark hit 35 home runs in his second year and batted .308. No Giants player had hit 30 homers and batted .300 since Hall of Fame first baseman Willie McCovey did so in 1969.

In 1988, Clark's third year in the majors, he led the league with 100 walks and 109 RBIs. The following year he was the MVP runner-up. He led the league in runs with 104, finished second in batting (.333), hits (196) and total bases (321), and third in RBIs (111), triples (9) and slugging percentage (.546). On top of that, he batted .472 with two home runs and eight RBIs in the playoffs and World Series.

Clark studies pitchers with the same intensity as Orel Hershiser examines hitters. He has videotapes of every pitcher he has faced, and he studies them during the off-season. Because he has done his homework, he is rarely surprised at the plate. Clark is exactly what a manager wants from the third hitter in his lineup: a big run-producer who hits for average and power.

Andre Dawson

It seems hard to believe now, but in 1987, Dawson—who that year would hit 49 home runs and win the MVP Award—went begging for a major league contract. He signed with the Cubs only after he gave them a blank contract and told them to fill in his salary. He played that year for $500,000, after earning $1.1 million the year before.

We know now that Dawson was nearly kept from playing because of a plot by the major league owners to keep salaries down. Had he been forced to sit out a season, it would have been a shame—both for him and for baseball fans. Dawson has been one of the top players of the last 15 years. He has whacked more than 300 home runs and more than 2,000 hits. In 1987, his MVP year, he led the National League with 137 RBIs.

Dawson has ranked among the top 10 in the league in batting average four times. He has won eight Gold Glove Awards, a feat only six other outfielders have achieved. Through 1989, he had played in five All-Star Games.

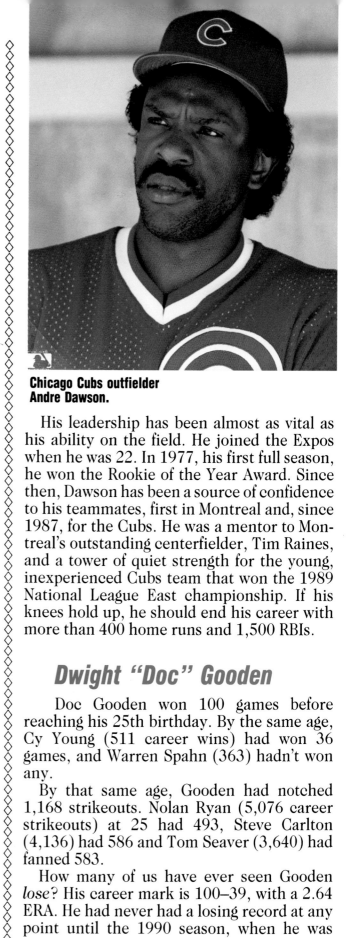

Chicago Cubs outfielder Andre Dawson.

His leadership has been almost as vital as his ability on the field. He joined the Expos when he was 22. In 1977, his first full season, he won the Rookie of the Year Award. Since then, Dawson has been a source of confidence to his teammates, first in Montreal and, since 1987, for the Cubs. He was a mentor to Montreal's outstanding centerfielder, Tim Raines, and a tower of quiet strength for the young, inexperienced Cubs team that won the 1989 National League East championship. If his knees hold up, he should end his career with more than 400 home runs and 1,500 RBIs.

Dwight "Doc" Gooden

Doc Gooden won 100 games before reaching his 25th birthday. By the same age, Cy Young (511 career wins) had won 36 games, and Warren Spahn (363) hadn't won any.

By that same age, Gooden had notched 1,168 strikeouts. Nolan Ryan (5,076 career strikeouts) at 25 had 493, Steve Carlton (4,136) had 586 and Tom Seaver (3,640) had fanned 583.

How many of us have ever seen Gooden *lose?* His career mark is 100–39, with a 2.64 ERA. He had never had a losing record at any point until the 1990 season, when he was recovering from arm surgery. He burst into prominence in 1984 as a 19-year-old rookie with the Mets. He went 17–9 with a 2.60 ERA and 276 strikeouts—a record for a rookie. Mets fans went crazy. They had never seen anyone like him. They nicknamed him "Dr. K," and started hanging big "K" signs from the stands for every one of his strikeouts.

The next year, 1985, he was even better, going 24–4 with a 1.53 ERA and 268 strike-

outs. He became the youngest pitcher ever to win both the Cy Young Award and 20 games in a season.

Gooden nearly threw his career away in 1987. He started using cocaine. But during spring training that season, he went to doctors to get help getting off the drug. He returned to the Mets in June and went 15–7 for the remainder of the year.

Gooden now knows how fleeting and fragile

Dwight Gooden, the youngest player to win both the Cy Young Award and 20 games in a season.

even the greatest talent can be, and he has rededicated himself to his career. He could be the greatest ever. The Mets have a history of trading away their greatest pitchers—in past years they've unloaded Tom Seaver, Nolan Ryan and Mike Scott—but Mets fans don't ever want to say goodbye to Doc.

Orel Hershiser

In 1983, his rookie year with the Dodgers, Hershiser was so unsure of himself that manager Tommy Lasorda had to lecture him not to give up. Now his teammates call him "Bulldog." He lived up to that nickname in 1988 when he pitched a record 59 consecutive shutout innings and led the Dodgers to the pennant and a World Series victory.

Hershiser's 1988 season was one of the best in recent history. On top of the scoreless inning streak, he went 23–8, with eight shutouts and a 2.26 ERA. He was the unanimous winner of the league's Cy Young Award, and was named the Most Valuable Player for both the playoffs and the World Series. *Sports Illustrated* named him Sportsman of the Year.

Hershiser succeeds because of an excellent sinker and pinpoint control—and because he studies opposing batters more carefully than any pitcher in the game. He maintains computerized records of every National League batter to help him decide what pitches to throw, and where in the strike zone to place them.

Ryne Sandberg

You look at Ryne and think of a Boy Scout. He is quiet, diligent, humble, polite—everything a Scout should be.

Of course, that's not how National League managers look at Sandberg. They see him as one of the greatest second basemen in the history of the game. They see a player who in 1989 hit 30 home runs and played errorless ball for a record 90 games in a row. It's hard to believe he came to the Cubs from the Phillies in 1982 as partial payment for shortstop Ivan DeJesus.

Sandberg was the rising star who carried the Cubs to their 1984 division title, and the steadying leader who led them to a second title in 1989. He was the league MVP in 1984,

Ryne Sandberg, one of the greatest second basemen ever.

with 200 hits, a .314 average and a league-leading 114 runs and 19 triples. In 1989, he became the first second baseman to hit 30 home runs since Davey Johnson did it for the Braves in 1973. He also became the first second baseman in National League history to win seven straight Gold Gloves. Only Pittsburgh's Bill Mazeroski and Kansas City's Frank White, with eight each, have won more. His .989 career fielding percentage is the best in history at his position.

Sandberg was 21 when he was called up to the Phillies in September of 1981. That winter he was traded to the Cubs and has played for Chicago ever since. He has appeared in six straight All-Star Games. He is "Mr. Dependable" for the Cubs. Quietly, steadily, he is playing his way into the Hall of Fame.

Ozzie Smith

It is the fourth inning, two out, the San Diego Padres against the Atlanta Braves in San Diego in 1978. Braves outfielder Jeff Burroughs hits a sharp grounder up the middle. Shortstop Ozzie Smith, the "Wizard of Oz," sprints and then dives, arms stretched out, to his left. At the last instant, the ball takes a bad hop high into the air. Ozzie, in the middle of his dive, reaches up with his bare hand and catches the ball, and then throws Burroughs out at first.

Ozzie says it's his favorite play. Perhaps you have another stored away in your mind, ready to turn to whenever you're in need of inspiration. Ozzie turns them out like clockwork. It's possible that he is the greatest fielding shortstop—or the greatest fielder, period—in history.

Only two players have won the Gold Glove Award every year in a decade. The first was Hall of Fame third-baseman Brooks Robinson, who swept the fielding awards in the 1960s. The second was Ozzie, in the 1980s. The 10 Gold Glove Awards he had won through 1989 are the most ever for a shortstop.

But Smith is more than just an amazing fielder. Through hard work, he transformed himself from a .220 hitter early in his career to an offensive threat who batted .303 in 1987, switch-hitting. He has also stolen more than 400 bases.

Smith joined the Padres in 1978, when he

Ozzie Smith, the "Wizard of Oz," shortstop for the Cardinals.

was 23. In one of the biggest trades of the 1980s, San Diego shipped him to St. Louis after the 1981 season for All-Star shortstop Garry Templeton. Smith has played for the Cardinals ever since. He has made the All-Star team nine times.

Go to the ballpark or turn on the television and watch him. You owe it to yourself. It's hard to imagine there will ever be a better shortstop.

Darryl Strawberry

Even his name is special: Darryl Strawberry. In terms of talent, he appears to be the batting equivalent of Gooden. When Strawberry plays at his best, few play the game better. In his first seven seasons, he hit 215 home runs and stole 176 bases. He is the only National Leaguer in history to be voted a starter on the All-Star team his first four full years in the majors. He has been the Mets rightfielder since 1983, when he was 21.

He is truly menacing at the plate. Strawberry is 6'6", with arms like an octopus and wrists like steel cables. He swings in a tremendous, uppercutting arc, and when he connects, you can hurt your neck following the ball out of the park. At his best, in 1987, he smashed 39 homers while driving in 104 runs, scoring 108 runs and stealing 36 bases. Even at his worst, in 1989, he hit 29 home runs. Strawberry could be one of the great players of the 1990s.

Power hitter Darryl Strawberry.

Kansas City Royals George Brett.

THE BEST OF THE AMERICAN LEAGUE:

George Brett

The chase of a glorious, seemingly unattainable achievement is the most dramatic thing in sports. In 1961, an entire nation followed Roger Maris as he approached Babe Ruth's single-season record of 60 home runs. Seventeen years later, Pete Rose's 44-game hitting streak dominated the news. In 1980, fans held their breath and rooted for Kansas City's George Brett to bat .400.

On August 17, Brett went above the .400 mark for the first time. Nine days later, he went 5-for-5 against the Milwaukee Brewers to lift his average to .407. He was still batting .400 as late as September 19. Then, sadly, he ran out of steam. Brett finished the season batting .390, the highest anyone had hit since Ted Williams reached .406 in 1941.

Brett's achievement was hardly a fluke. He is among the finest hitters of this era, winning two batting titles and topping .300 10 times. His career average, through 1989 and 17 big-league seasons, was .310.

Brett was named to 14 consecutive All-Star Games, more than any current player. During his career, he has led the league three times in hits, triples and slugging average, and once each in doubles, on-base percentage and total bases.

Brett won the 1980 MVP Award. Pitchers hold him in such awe that in 1985 they intentionally walked him 31 times, just two short of Ted Williams's American League record. Through 1989, Brett had collected 2,528 hits.

Brett joined the Royals in 1973, when he was 20, and has played for them ever since. He played third base most of his career and won a Gold Glove there in 1985. He moved to first base in 1987.

Jose Canseco

Forget the videotapes of Bo Jackson breaking bats over his helmet; Canseco is the strongest man in the game. He once hit a home run in spring training that went right *through* the outfield fence. He is 6′3″ and 230 pounds, and built like Mr. Universe.

Pitchers know all this. In his first three full years in the majors, the Oakland rightfielder cracked 106 home runs. Over the same period, he drove in 354 runs, an average of 118 per season. In 1988, he led the league with 42 homers and 124 RBIs, and was voted the league's MVP. That year, he also stole 40 bases, becoming the first player in history to steal 40 bases and hit 40 homers in the same year.

Canseco arrived in Oakland at the tail end of the 1985 season, when he was 21. He struck out on three pitches in his first at bat. In fact, he fanned 12 times in his first 24 trips to the plate. After two weeks, though, he turned things around. His second major league homer cleared the roof at Comiskey Park. He ended the season batting .302.

Since then, he has been unstoppable. In 1988, he ranked in the top 10 in 12 of baseball's major hitting categories. Twenty-seven of his 42 homers that year either tied the game or put Oakland ahead. If he stays healthy there's no telling how high his game can soar.

Roger "The Rocket" Clemens

"The Rocket" was clocked throwing 100 miles per hour against Detroit. Not even Dwight Gooden is that fast. Gooden fanned 1,168 from 1984 through 1989. Over the same period, Clemens struck out 1,215. The Red Sox righthander fanned 230 batters in 1989, and that was his lowest total in four years.

Clemens has so many big numbers, but his single most impressive number is 20. That's how many Seattle Mariners he struck out April 29, 1986, in a nine-inning ballgame. No one has ever struck out that many players in a single game. Afterward, the Mariners said that Clemens had been in another zone, completely unhittable. His fastball jumped so sharply that it was nearly impossible to follow. Almost as amazing as his strikeout total that night was the number of walks he issued: 0. That's what makes Clemens so dominating—he is a 6′4″, 220-pound Texan with an other-worldly fastball and pinpoint control.

He joined the Boston Red Sox in 1984, when he was 21. His first two years were shortened by injuries. In 1986, his first full season, Clemens went 24–4 and had a league-leading ERA of 2.48. He started the year 14–0. He didn't lose until July 2. Batters that year hit .195 against him. He won the Cy Young and MVP Awards, and was named Most Valuable Player of the All-Star Game. In 1987, he won the Cy Young Award again, with a 20–9 record. He was 16–3 over his last 23 starts that season. His career record through 1989 was a Gooden-like 95–45. He is already one of the best Red Sox pitchers ever.

Carlton "Pudge" Fisk

When you think of "Pudge" Fisk, you should think of him standing at home plate, in the 12th inning of the sixth game of the 1975 World Series at Boston's Fenway Park, arms above his head, trying with body English to keep his towering fly over the leftfield wall from going foul. And when he succeeds, you see him leaping in the air like he had just won the lottery and then circling the bases, still clapping his hands. Fisk's homer was possibly the most dramatic in the history of the World Series.

Rickey Henderson setting a stolen base record.

It's almost as incredible to realize that so many years later, Fisk is still playing. And not just playing, but starting and catching well.

Fisk has caught more major league games than any man except Bob Boone. Through 1989, he had hit 336 home runs, more than any catcher except Johnny Bench and Yogi Berra. He had 117 career stolen bases, and is the only catcher in history to top 100 in both stolen bases and home runs. He has played on 10 All-Star teams.

Fisk, in his 40s, is still able to catch because of his adherence to a grueling off-season training regimen. No one has ever worked harder to stay in shape. His Chicago White Sox teammates hold him in awe.

The grim New Englander joined the Boston Red Sox in 1969. In 1981, he became a free agent, signed with the White Sox, and has played with them ever since.

Through 1989, Fisk had 2,063 hits, 1,166 RBIs, 1,155 runs and a .271 lifetime batting average. He already has the credentials for the Hall of Fame.

Rickey Henderson

Rickey Henderson is the greatest leadoff hitter in the history of the game. In 1988, a typical season for Henderson, he batted .305 and stole 93 bases. Leading games off, he went 37 for 120 for a .308 average. He reached base safely another 19 times via walks and errors. Forty of those 56 times, he scored! From July 18 through August 3, he reached first base safely leading off in 15 straight games. Eleven of *those* times, he scored.

There's more. Unlike most speed burners, such as Vince Coleman and Gerald Young, Henderson possesses real power. Through 1989, he had led off games with a home run 40 times, a major league record. In 1986, he swatted 28 home runs and drove in 74 runs. In 1985, he did almost as well, hitting 24 homers and knocking home 72 runs.

By the time you read this, Henderson most likely will have broken Lou Brock's career record of 938 stolen bases. He already holds the season record, having swiped 130 in 1982.

Two other times he has stolen 100 or more. He led the American League in stealing nine times during the 1980s.

Henderson is almost impossible to pitch to. He bats from an extreme crouch, providing a strike zone that appears no bigger than the ball itself. Walk him, as pitchers have done an average of 91 times a year, and you set him loose on the bases. Pitch to him, and you'll likely put him on base anyway: Henderson boasts a career .290 average. He has scored 100 or more runs eight times in his 11-year career.

He began his career in Oakland in 1979. He was traded to the Yankees after the 1984 season, and traded back to Oakland in mid-1989. Yes, he's cocky, but until somebody figures out a way to stop him, he'll continue to have his say.

Don Mattingly

Almost hidden behind the noise of owner George Steinbrenner and the bluster of managers such as Billy Martin and Dallas Green is the fact that Don Mattingly is the best first baseman the New York Yankees—or any other American League team—has had since Lou Gehrig.

It's hard to exaggerate how good Don Mattingly is. Through 1989 and after eight years in the majors, his career average was .323—better than any of his fellow big leaguers except Boggs, Gwynn and Puckett. He drove in 684 runs in the six seasons from 1984 to 1989—a phenomenal average of 114 per year. In that same period of time, he collected 1,219 hits, an average of 203 a season. Not even Yankees owner George Steinbrenner can gripe about that.

There's more: He hit six grand slam homers in 1987, a major league record. He tied another record that season by hitting at least one home run a game for eight straight games. In 1986, he tallied 238 hits. That year he became the first American League player ever to whack 230 hits, 30 home runs and 100 RBIs. He also hit 53 doubles, becoming the first player to lead the American League in doubles for three consecutive years since Cleveland centerfielder Tris Speaker led the league from 1920 to 1923 (four straight years). In 1985, the year he was the league MVP, he drove in 145 runs—the most by a Yankee since Joe DiMaggio knocked in 155 in 1948. In 1984 he won the batting title by batting .343.

As if his batting prowess weren't enough, he also won five consecutive Gold Glove Awards.

Yankees Don Mattingly, the best first baseman since Lou Gehrig.

59

Minnesota Twins Kirby Puckett.

Kirby Puckett

From 1987 to 1989, Wade Boggs, Tony Gwynn and Kirby Puckett won every major league batting championship. What's the difference between them? Boggs and Gwynn are singles hitters. Puckett has the power to hit 30 home runs in a year, and from 1986 to 1989 averaged 100 RBIs.

When Puckett started out, no one except a few Minnesota scouts suspected he had such power. In 1984, his rookie year, Puckett appeared at the plate 573 times and hit no homers. Two years later, after getting some confidence in his swing, he socked 31 home runs. He has hit with power ever since.

Puckett won his first batting title in 1989, when he batted .339 to beat out Wade Boggs for the crown. In the four seasons from 1986 to 1989, Puckett never batted lower than .328. His .356 average in 1988 was the highest in the American League by a righthanded hitter since Joe DiMaggio reached .357 in 1941. He has had at least 207 hits in each of the last four years, and is only the fourth player ever to reach the 1,000-hit mark in his fifth season.

Perhaps the most surprising of Puckett's abilities is his fielding. He is an acrobat in centerfield, despite being built like a small refrigerator. He is 5'8" and weighs 210 pounds. Puckett has won four Gold Glove Awards, and he has perhaps the strongest arm in the league.

The stubby outfielder joined the Minnesota Twins in 1984 and has played for them ever since. Through 1989, his career average was .323. His short, quick, powerful stroke should ensure many more .300 seasons.

Cal Ripken, Jr.

Four and a half more years. Going into the 1990 season, Cal Ripken, Jr. had played 1,250 straight games, the second longest consecutive-game streak in history. He began it May 30, 1982. If he plays every ballgame until mid-1995, he'll break Lou Gehrig's record of 2,130 straight games.

It's one thing to play every game, and another to play every game *well*. That's what makes Ripken's attempt special. He is not Lou

In his first six full seasons, he had more total hits than Pete Rose, Stan Musial, Ted Williams, Lou Gehrig or Babe Ruth did in their first six seasons.

Mattingly began with the Yankees in 1982, when he was 21. He has been their first baseman ever since, the one rock in a sea of constant change.

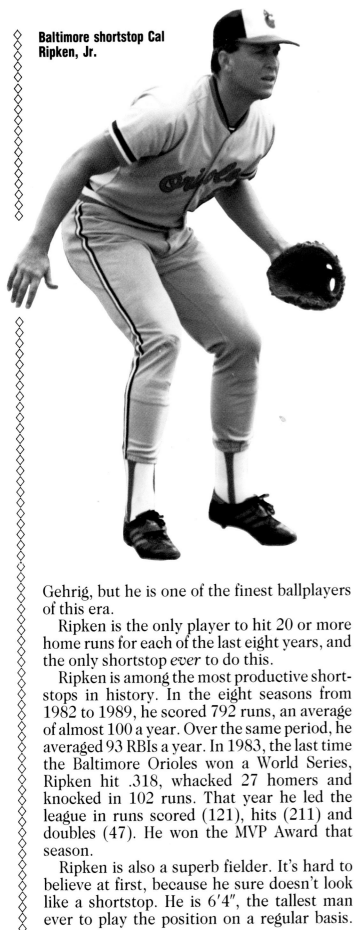

Through 1989, he had led American League shortstops in assists four times in the previous six years. In 1989, he led all major league shortstops in total chances, putouts, assists and double plays. He isn't fast or flashy, but he has an accurate arm. He played in seven All-Star Games during the 1980s.

Ripken first made the Orioles roster when he was 21, and he has played for them ever since. By his 30th birthday, he had passed 1,500 career hits. He has a chance to get 3,000 hits if he remains healthy. That, and his playing streak, should put him in the Hall of Fame.

Nolan Ryan

Do you need a fastball? Nolan Ryan is by far and away the greatest strikeout pitcher in the history of the game. Through 1989, he had fanned 5,076 batters, 940 more than Steve Carlton, his nearest competitor. His lifetime record stood at 289–263.

When discussing Ryan, the question is where to start? He holds the single-season strikeout record—383, which he set in 1973. He has averaged 9.54 strikeouts per nine innings over his career. Sandy Koufax, with 9.28 per game, is the only other pitcher to average more than one strikeout per inning. In 1987, Ryan averaged 11.48 strikeouts per nine innings, the highest single-season figure in history.

Ryan has six seasons of 300 or more strikeouts and 13 seasons of 200 or more. Both of those marks are major league records. (There have been just 22 300-plus strikeout seasons in all of baseball history.) Through 1989, Ryan had fanned 10 or more hitters in a game 199 times. He struck out 19 in a game four times. Ryan has won 10 strikeout titles. Only Walter Johnson won more (12).

Ryan struck out 301 batters in 1989, when he was 42. He has added an excellent changeup to a fastball that still clocks 95 miles per hour and a sharp curve. Ryan has become even tougher to hit as he approaches middle age. He threw two one-hitters in 1989, and five times took no-hitters into the eighth inning. Of course, that is nothing new for Ryan. He has thrown a major league record six no-hitters. Through 1989, he had also thrown

Gehrig, but he is one of the finest ballplayers of this era.

Ripken is the only player to hit 20 or more home runs for each of the last eight years, and the only shortstop *ever* to do this.

Ripken is among the most productive shortstops in history. In the eight seasons from 1982 to 1989, he scored 792 runs, an average of almost 100 a year. Over the same period, he averaged 93 RBIs a year. In 1983, the last time the Baltimore Orioles won a World Series, Ripken hit .318, whacked 27 homers and knocked in 102 runs. That year he led the league in runs scored (121), hits (211) and doubles (47). He won the MVP Award that season.

Ripken is also a superb fielder. It's hard to believe at first, because he sure doesn't look like a shortstop. He is 6'4", the tallest man ever to play the position on a regular basis.

11 one-hitters over the course of a 23-year career.

In 1966, when Ryan was 19, he was promoted to the Mets. He was traded to the Angels after the 1971 season. He signed with Houston as a free agent in 1980, and signed with Texas as a free agent after the 1988 season. Ryan says he can pitch a few more years. Who knows? Maybe he can pitch until he's 50. By then, perhaps his fastball will have slowed down to 85 mph—which would still be as fast as the average major league heater.

The greatest strikeout pitcher in baseball, Nolan Ryan.

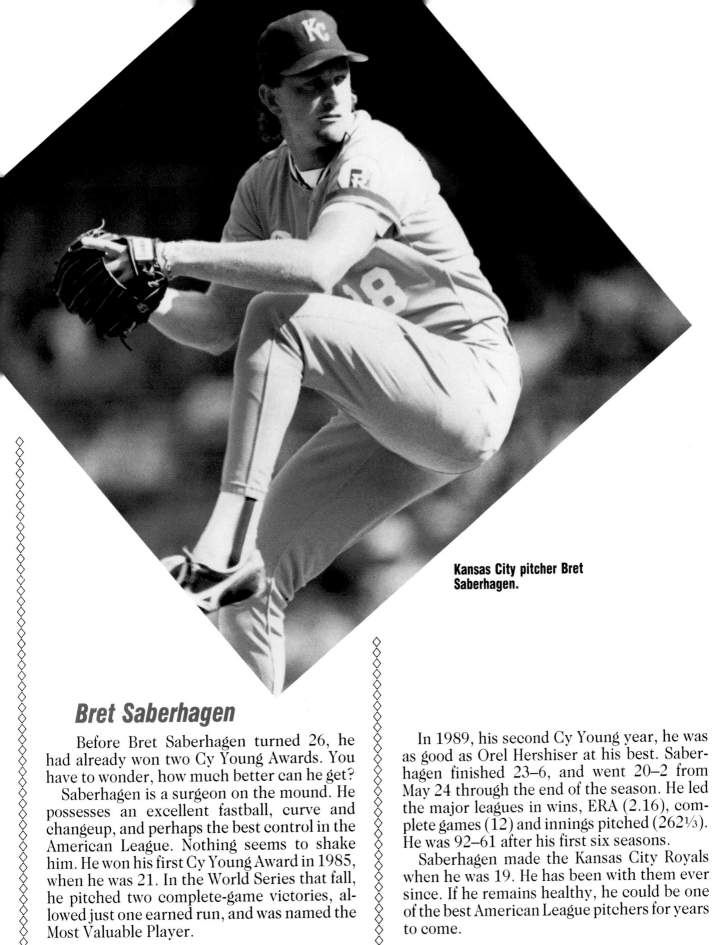

Kansas City pitcher Bret Saberhagen.

Bret Saberhagen

Before Bret Saberhagen turned 26, he had already won two Cy Young Awards. You have to wonder, how much better can he get?

Saberhagen is a surgeon on the mound. He possesses an excellent fastball, curve and changeup, and perhaps the best control in the American League. Nothing seems to shake him. He won his first Cy Young Award in 1985, when he was 21. In the World Series that fall, he pitched two complete-game victories, allowed just one earned run, and was named the Most Valuable Player.

In 1989, his second Cy Young year, he was as good as Orel Hershiser at his best. Saberhagen finished 23–6, and went 20–2 from May 24 through the end of the season. He led the major leagues in wins, ERA (2.16), complete games (12) and innings pitched (262⅓). He was 92–61 after his first six seasons.

Saberhagen made the Kansas City Royals when he was 19. He has been with them ever since. If he remains healthy, he could be one of the best American League pitchers for years to come.

CHAPTER 6

HALL OF FAME PLAYERS

We learn a lot about baseball through listening. Baseball is sharing stories between father and son, mother and daughter, between brothers, sisters and friends. One way we judge Rickey Henderson's talent is to hear others talk about Lou Brock or Maury Wills or Ty Cobb. One way we appreciate Dwight Gooden is to listen to others recount stories about Bob Gibson or Bob Feller or Walter "Big Train" Johnson. Over 25,000 men have played major league baseball; just 181 have been good enough to be elected to the Hall of Fame. Here are a few of the best.

Hank Aaron

Aaron did the impossible. He broke Babe Ruth's career home run record. He hit number 714 in his first at bat of the 1974 season to tie Ruth, and then hit the record-breaker a few days later before his hometown Atlanta Braves fans. (Los Angeles Dodgers Al Downing will always be a trivia answer as the pitcher who yielded Aaron the historic home run.) By the time Hank retired in 1976, he had walloped an incredible 755 homers.

Unlike other great sluggers, Aaron never hit 50 home runs in a season. His high was 47. He topped Ruth slowly, by whacking 30 or more homers 15 times, and 40 or more eight times in his 23-year career. He won four home run championships and whacked 16 grand slams along the way.

Aaron did other things besides hit home runs. He holds the major league records for RBIs (2,297), total bases (6,856) and extra-base hits (1,477). He ranks third in hits, with 3,771, and runs, with 2,174. Aaron twice led the league in hitting and finished with a .305 career average. He won the Most Valuable Player Award in 1957. He also won three Gold Gloves for his play in the outfield.

Aaron entered the league in 1954. He played 21 years for the Milwaukee, and then Atlanta Braves, and retired in 1976 after two seasons with the Milwaukee Brewers. He was elected to the Hall of Fame in 1981.

Ty Cobb

Ty Cobb was without question the greatest hitter and the most feared base runner the game has ever known. He was to singles hitters what Babe Ruth was to sluggers. His record of 4,191 hits stood for 57 years until Pete Rose broke it in 1985.

Yet he was also one of the roughest, nastiest men to play the game. Think of Ty Cobb and you think of him sliding, spikes high, into the second baseman. You think of shouting and intimidation. He always seemed to be daring the opposition to beat him. He was born in 1886 in rural Narrows, Georgia, where even as a child he was a fierce competitor in every way. There was no mistaking his presence on the field.

Despite his nasty disposition, Ty Cobb was the greatest hitter baseball has ever known.

Though Cobb was not a home run hitter, he had his share of extra-base hits. He hit the second-most triples in history, 297, and the fourth-most doubles, 724. He ranks first in career runs scored with 2,245 and fourth in career RBIs with 1,961.

Cobb's cunning on the bases was as impressive as his hitting. He stole 96 bases in 1915, a record that stood for 47 years. And even now, with speedsters like Rickey Henderson and Vince Coleman in the game, Cobb ranks third all-time with 892 stolen bases.

Cobb became Detroit's playing manager in 1921, and remained at the helm of the club through 1926. He played his last two years for the Philadelphia Athletics, and retired in 1928. Eight years later he was elected to the Hall of Fame. He died in 1961.

Joe DiMaggio

"The Yankee Clipper" was perhaps the most graceful, elegant player the game has known. He had a style and presence that both teammates and fans recognized and appreciated. He seemed born to roam Yankee Stadium's centerfield. The New York Yankees considered him so vital, they offered him $100,000 (the top salary in 1952) to postpone his retirement and just play their home games. (He declined the offer.)

DiMaggio was among the game's greatest natural hitters. He hit better than .300 in 11 of his 13 seasons, and led the league twice in batting. His top mark was .381 in 1939. His career mark was .325. He won the Most Valuable Player Award in 1939, 1941 and 1947.

Of all the great batting records that once seemed unapproachable—Babe Ruth's 60 home runs in a season and 714 home runs lifetime, Ty Cobb's 4,191 hits—only DiMaggio's 56-game hitting streak in 1941 has stood the test of time. "Joltin' Joe" hit safely in 56 games in a row! Pete Rose and Willie Keeler are second with 44 games.

DiMaggio was a fearsome slugger. He smacked 361 homers, despite missing three of his prime playing years while in the armed services during World War II. Twice he led the American League in home runs. His .579 career slugging average is the sixth highest in the game, ahead of Willie Mays, Mickey Mantle and Hank Aaron.

Cobb joined the Detroit Tigers in 1905 when he was 18. In 1907, his first season as the regular centerfielder for the Tigers, he led the American League in hits with 212 and in batting average at .350. That was the first of nine straight years he would lead the American League with his batting average. He won the title 12 times altogether. Eight times he led the league in hits; nine times he topped 200 hits in a season. In 1911 he stroked 248 hits and batted .420. That was one of three times Cobb batted .400 in a season. His lifetime batting average was .367, the best in history. Mickey Mantle, Willie Mays and Pete Rose *never* batted .367 for one season.

New York's "Yankee Clipper" Joe DiMaggio.

DiMaggio joined the Yankees in 1936, when he was 21. The Yanks held onto him for his entire 13-year major league career. He retired in 1951. Four years later, he was elected to the Hall of Fame.

Lou Gehrig

Gehrig was quite simply the finest first baseman who ever lived. For most of his 17-year career (1923–1939) with the New York Yankees, he batted cleanup behind the Babe. Of all the great slugging duos—Will Clark and Kevin Mitchell, Jose Canseco and Mark McGwire, Mickey Mantle and Roger Maris—none has ever equaled Ruth and Gehrig. In the 1920s and 1930s, they were baseball's twin towers of greatness.

Gehrig hit 493 home runs in his career, the 15th most in history. (When Gehrig retired, he and Ruth were the top two home run batters in history.) He won three home run titles, and for the seven years from 1930 to 1936, he averaged 40 homers a season. In 1927, the year Ruth hit 60 home runs, Gehrig smacked 47. In 1932, he hit four home runs in one nine-inning game. His 23 grand slams are by far the most in history.

Gehrig's career slugging average of .632 ranks third, after Ruth and Ted Williams. His 1,990 RBIs also rank third. In 1931, he drove in 184 runs, the American League record for a single season. Four times, he knocked in 165 runs or more. The last time anyone drove in 150 was 1962.

His lifetime batting average was .340. Gehrig batted .300 for 12 straight years, including a league-leading .363 in 1934.

But the record Gehrig was most proud of was his consecutive game playing streak. On June 1, 1925, Gehrig made a pinch-hitting appearance. The next day he replaced Wally Pipp at first base and he remained in the lineup every single game for the next 13½ years! He played in 2,130 consecutive games, a streak that earned him his nickname, "the Iron Horse."

Gehrig, who attended Columbia University, was one of the most decent, liked and admired men to play the game. His career was sadly cut short in 1939 by amyotrophic lateral sclerosis (ALS), today more commonly known as Lou Gehrig's Disease. In 1939, he was elected to the Hall of Fame. He died just two years later, at the age of 37.

Sandy Koufax

For five years, beginning in 1962, Sandy Koufax was perhaps the most dominating pitcher in the history of the game. He led the league in ERA each of those years, and topped the league in wins three times, with 25 in 1963, 26 in 1965, and 27 in 1966. Then, at the age of 30, he suddenly retired because of the arthritis that wracked his left arm.

Koufax was a southpaw (lefthander) with a rocket fastball and a devastating overhand curve. He pitched seven years for the Dodgers before fully mastering his control. But when he did, he was nearly unhittable. He pitched four no-hitters in four years, including a 1–0 perfect game victory over the Chicago Cubs in 1965. In 1965, Koufax allowed a mere 5.79 hits per nine innings. He pitched 11 shutouts in 1963 alone. Three times his ERA was under 1.90.

In five seasons, Koufax averaged more than 10 strikeouts per nine innings. Three times he fanned over 300 batters in a season. In 1965, Koufax struck out 382. Only Nolan Ryan has matched him as a strikeout pitcher.

Koufax's record from 1962 through 1966 was 111–34. For his 12-year career, all with the Dodgers, he was 165–87. His .655 winning percentage ranks 10th in history. In 1972, he was elected to the Hall of Fame.

The southpaw with a killer fastball, Dodgers Sandy Koufax.

Mickey Mantle

Mickey Mantle arrived to play centerfield for the New York Yankees just as Joe DiMaggio was leaving. In 12 of his first 14 years with the team, the Yankees reached the World Series. He was ballyhooed as the greatest player to enter the game, and, despite serious leg injuries, he very nearly was.

Mantle was the greatest switch-hitter the game has known. (A switch-hitter can bat from either side of the plate, both lefthanded and righthanded.) Three times he won the American League's Most Valuable Player Award, in 1956, 1957 and 1962. He won the Triple Crown in 1956, with 52 home runs, 130 RBIs and a .353 batting average.

The chunky, blond Oklahoman hit some of the longest home runs in history. One was measured at 565 feet. He won four home run titles, and hit 536 round-trippers in all, the eighth most in history. In 1961, the year Roger Maris hit a record 61 homers, Mantle whacked 54. He was so feared as a hitter, pitchers walked him 1,734 times, more than anyone except Babe Ruth and Ted Williams.

Mantle hit a World Series record 18 home runs, and also holds the Series marks for most RBIs and runs scored.

He joined the Yankees in 1951, when he was 19, and remained with them until he retired in 1968. He was elected to the Hall of Fame in 1974.

Christy Mathewson

He was the Lou Gehrig of pitchers, intelligent, soft-spoken, ethical—and among the best there was at his craft.

Mathewson won 373 games from 1900 to 1916, all but one of those victories coming for the New York Giants. Only Cy Young and Walter "Big Train" Johnson won more games. Matty had an excellent fastball and a remarkable fadeaway, which we now call a screwball. He also had superb confidence and pinpoint control; he averaged just 1.58 walks per nine innings and he fanned 2,502. In 1913, he pitched 68 consecutive innings without allowing a single walk. Twice he pitched no-hitters.

Mathewson won 22 games or more for 12 straight years; he won 30 or more four times,

including 37 wins in 1908. His lifetime ERA was 2.13, the fifth best in history. By comparison, in 1989, Bret Saberhagen had the lowest ERA in either league at 2.16. Mathewson led the league in ERA five times. In 1909, a year in which he went 25–6, his ERA was 1.14.

Like Cy Young, Mathewson generally finished what he started. He threw 435 complete games, 80 of them shutouts. Only Walter Johnson and Grover Alexander had more shutouts. In the 1905 World Series, Matty pitched three shutouts against the Athletics in what is still the best Series pitching performance ever.

Matty ended his career with the Cincinnati Reds in 1916. He managed the Reds for the next 2½ years and then retired from baseball. He was one of the few players to take an active stand against the gambling and game-fixing that eventually led to the 1919 Black Sox scandal. He was elected to the Hall of Fame in 1936. When Mathewson died in 1925, he was just 45.

Willie Mays

Willie Mays, Mickey Mantle. Mickey Mantle, Willie Mays. Who was better? It was an unanswerable question that led to arguments for a whole generation of New Yorkers. Mays joined the New York Giants in 1951, the same year Mantle made the Yankees. Each played centerfield with style. Each ranked with the game's greatest power hitters. Each was the center of a champion team.

One could argue that Mantle's finest years were better than Mays's best. But perhaps because Mays remained free of injuries, he compiled more impressive career totals.

The "Say Hey Kid" won the Most Valuable Player Award two times, in 1954 and 1965. He was one of the finest and speediest centerfielders in history. Mays's historic 1954 catch of Vic Wertz's long line drive was celebrated because it was in the World Series, but Mays made many catches over the years that were equally spectacular.

Willie's hitting was no secret. He walloped 660 home runs; only Hank Aaron and Babe Ruth hit more. Twice he belted over 50 home-runs in a season, and four times he won the National League long ball championship. In

St. Louis Cardinals Stan Musial.

the five years from 1961 to 1965, Willie averaged 45 round-trippers a year.

Mays ranks seventh all-time with 1,903 RBIs. Ten times he drove in more than 100 runs in a season. He finished fourth with 1,323 extra-base hits and fifth with 2,062 runs. His lifetime average over 22 years was .302.

Mays played 21 years for the Giants, and finished his career with the New York Mets in 1973, at age 42. He was elected to the Hall of Fame in 1979.

Stan Musial

"Stan the Man" was the St. Louis Cardinals' answer to Ted Williams. The two were contemporaries. Musial joined the Cardinals in 1941, two years after Williams made the Red Sox. Both were outfielders (though Musial spent 7 of his 22 seasons mainly at first base), both were lefthanded power hitters with remarkable batting eyes, and each lost playing time to the armed forces (Musial missed 1945). Though fans were in awe of Williams, they were sometimes put off by his moods and his temper. Musial, however, was adored.

Fans loved him partly because he was humble and always generous with his time. Mostly, they loved him because The Man could hit. He batted over .300 18 times, and won seven batting championships. His lifetime average was .331.

Musial stroked 3,630 career hits, the fourth most in history. He hit 475 home runs along with 725 doubles—the third-highest number ever. Musial socked 1,377 extra-base hits, which is more than Babe Ruth hit and second only to Hank Aaron. He ranked fifth in RBIs (1,951), behind Aaron, Ruth, Gehrig and Cobb. His .559 career slugging average is the ninth best of all time. Three times he was voted the National League's Most Valuable Player.

Musial spent his entire career with the Cardinals. He retired in 1963, when he was 43. He was elected to the Hall of Fame in 1969.

Satchel Paige

A look at his slim major league record—28–31, 3.29 ERA—makes one wonder: What is he doing in the Hall of Fame? The truth is, had Leroy "Satchel" Paige not had to wait until he was 42 for a chance to pitch in the majors, he might have compiled the greatest record of all time.

For a long time, Paige couldn't pitch in the majors because he was black. He came of age before Jackie Robinson broke the color line in 1947, so he spent most of his career pitching for teams like the Pittsburgh Crawfords and the Kansas City Monarchs in the old Negro Leagues.

There are no authoritative records of how many games Paige won and lost in his 20 summers pitching in the Negro Leagues, and his 20 winters barnstorming across the United States, South America and the Caribbean. But, from time to time he pitched in exhibitions against major league all-stars, so they knew how great he was.

Paige was fast, but it was his remarkable control that set him apart. On his barnstorming tours, he would stick four long nails into a one-by-two inch plank, and prop it up behind home plate. Pitching from the mound, he

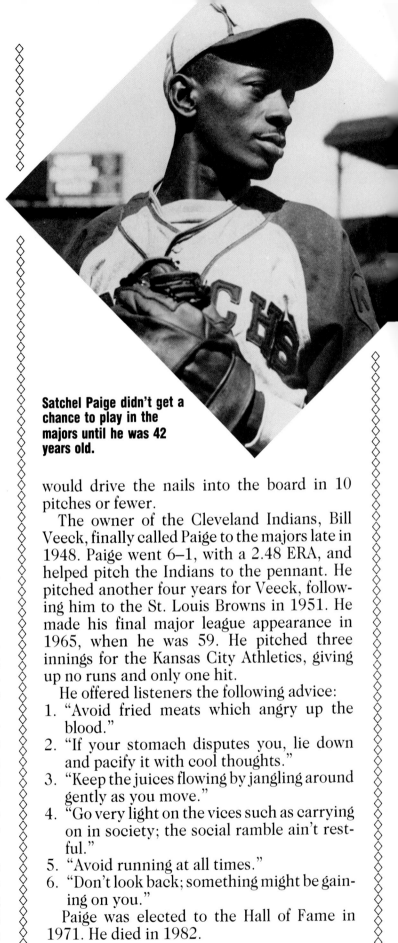

Satchel Paige didn't get a chance to play in the majors until he was 42 years old.

would drive the nails into the board in 10 pitches or fewer.

The owner of the Cleveland Indians, Bill Veeck, finally called Paige to the majors late in 1948. Paige went 6–1, with a 2.48 ERA, and helped pitch the Indians to the pennant. He pitched another four years for Veeck, following him to the St. Louis Browns in 1951. He made his final major league appearance in 1965, when he was 59. He pitched three innings for the Kansas City Athletics, giving up no runs and only one hit.

He offered listeners the following advice:

1. "Avoid fried meats which angry up the blood."
2. "If your stomach disputes you, lie down and pacify it with cool thoughts."
3. "Keep the juices flowing by jangling around gently as you move."
4. "Go very light on the vices such as carrying on in society; the social ramble ain't restful."
5. "Avoid running at all times."
6. "Don't look back; something might be gaining on you."

Paige was elected to the Hall of Fame in 1971. He died in 1982.

Babe Ruth

For starters, all the stories you've heard about the Babe are probably true. He was a barrel-chested, spindle-legged, flat-faced giant of a man whose appetite for food made almost as much news as his hitting. Ruth came to fame almost immediately after the 1919 Black Sox scandal, a larger-than-life hero who singlehandedly relit people's enthusiasm for the game.

The Babe was born George Herman Ruth in 1895 in Baltimore, Maryland, and grew up at St. Mary's Industrial School, a home for orphans and children who got in trouble. He remained there until he was 19, when he signed a $600-a-year contract with the minor league Baltimore Orioles. Sixteen years later, he was earning $80,000—more than the President of the United States was paid at the time.

He changed the very way the game was played. Ruth ushered out the age of the single hitters and turned baseball into a power-hitting game. As more and more people flocked to stadiums around the league to watch Ruth hit homers, owners of other teams tried to lure away the fans with sluggers of their own, but no other power hitter ever captured the fancy of the fans as the Babe did.

All the stories you've heard about the Babe's home runs are probably true, too. Roger Maris topped his single-season record of 60 homers in a season, and Hank Aaron beat his career mark of 714, but the Babe remains the sport's ultimate symbol of power.

Ruth hit baseballs higher and farther than anyone at the time even imagined possible. He launched them like giant meteors out of every ballpark in America. In 1919, a sportswriter wrote that one of his homers rose "into some floating white clouds" while the other team stood "transfixed with the splendor of it."

The Babe whacked 54 home runs in 1920, a year in which nobody else in the majors hit more than 19. In fact, that season he out-homered every *team* in the American League except his Yankees. His record 60 home runs in 154 games in 1927—the standard against which all hitting is still judged—stood for 34 years.

He topped the American League in home runs 12 times. He led six straight years, from 1926 to 1931, averaging 50 homers a year. Over his career, he averaged a home run every 11.8 at bats.

It may or may not be true, as some claimed, that he "called" his shot against the Chicago Cubs in the 1932 World Series, pointing to centerfield after two strikes, then clubbing the ball into that spot in the Wrigley Field bleachers. It's definitely true that only the Babe *could* have done it.

His career batting average was .342, his career slugging average a record .690. How good is that? Kevin Mitchell led the National League in 1989 with a slugging average of .635. In 1921, the year Ruth hit 59 homers, scored 177 runs and drove in 171 runs, his slugging average was .846. That wasn't even his best season. The year before, he had slugged .847.

In 1921, the Babe clubbed a record 119 extra-base hits. He was so feared as a hitter that in 1923 he was walked 170 times. In his career, he was walked a record 2,056 times.

Ruth's hitting ability was so awesome, we sometimes forget that he was almost as talented at pitching as he was at batting. He first played in the majors with the Boston Red Sox in 1914 when he was 19, and just two years later won 23 games and led the league with a 1.75 ERA. He faced Walter "Big Train" Johnson, widely considered the best pitcher of the day, eight times. Ruth won six, three of them by 1–0 scores, one of them decided on his own home run. He was 94–46 as a pitcher, and he was 3–0 with an 0.87 ERA in three World Series games. At one point, he pitched 29 consecutive scoreless World Series innings.

The Red Sox sold him to the Yankees in 1920 for the unheard-of sum of $125,000. Ruth quit the mound for the outfield because the Yankees knew he was worth more playing everyday than every few days. He played for the Yankees until they released him in 1934. He joined the Boston Braves briefly in 1935, and then retired. The Babe was elected to the Hall of Fame in 1936, and died in 1948.

Honus Wagner

"The Flying Dutchman" was probably the best shortstop who ever played in the big

"The Flying Dutchman," Honus Wagner.

leagues. He had tremendous range—hence his nickname—and a strong, accurate throwing arm. But what set Wagner apart was his bat.

He won the National League batting title eight times, including seven times between 1903 and 1911. He batted over .300 each of his first 17 years in the majors. Wagner played in an era when the ball was made differently and was considered "dead" (it didn't travel as far) and so he hit few home runs, but he possessed enormous speed and power. He had a barrel chest, thick hands and arms, and could run almost as well as Ty Cobb. He ranks third in career triples, with 252, fifth in doubles, with 651, and sixth in stolen bases, with 722. He led the league in stolen bases five times.

Wagner reached the majors with Louisville in 1897, when he was 23. He went to the Pittsburgh Pirates in 1900, and he remained with them until he retired in 1917. Wagner was elected to the Hall of Fame in 1936. He lived until 1955.

Ted Williams

Ted Williams missed all or parts of five seasons when he was a pilot in World War II and the Korean War. He won the Triple Crown in 1942 with 36 home runs, 137 RBIs and a .356 batting average. He spent the next three years in the Marines. In 1951 he belted 30 homers, knocked in 126 runs and batted .318, and then joined the Marines again. He averaged 32 home runs a year through 1951, so it's

The player with 511 career wins, Cy Young.

reasonable to speculate that he lost 150 homers while in the service. Yet, the Boston Red Sox leftfielder still hit 521 round-trippers, the tenth-most in history.

For many of the years that Joe DiMaggio was the star of the New York Yankees, Ted Williams was the hero of the Boston Red Sox. Williams was unparalleled at the plate. A tall, rangy, powerful lefthanded batter, he seemed never to be fooled by a pitch. He had remarkable 20/10 vision (normal eyesight is 20/20), and was able to follow curveballs and sliders much more quickly than other batters. His eyesight was so famous that umpires didn't like to call strikes on close pitches that Williams let pass. He led the American League in walks eight times, and totaled 2,019 in his career, second only to Babe Ruth.

No doubt about it, hitting was his game. He led the league in batting six times. He was the last player to reach .400, batting .406 in 1941. He batted .388 in 1957, at age 39. In 19 years, he batted under .316 just once. His .344 lifetime average is the sixth best in history.

Twice he was named the American League's Most Valuable Player. He is the only American Leaguer to have won two Triple Crowns, having done so in 1942 and '47. *The Sporting News* named him to its Major League All-Star team 13 times. His .634 career slugging average is the second only to Ruth's. He drove in 100 or more runs nine times; four times he was the league leader, and in 1949 he tallied 159.

Williams spent his entire 19-year career with the Red Sox. He joined them at age 20, in 1939. He homered in his final at bat in the closing days of the 1960 season. He was elected to the Hall of Fame in 1966.

Cy Young

Start with his 511 career wins. That's more games than Tom Seaver and Sandy Koufax won—*combined*. Young completed 751 games. That's more games than Nolan Ryan, a 23-year veteran, has pitched in *at all*. He threw 76 shutouts, more than Steve Carlton and Lefty Grove, *combined*. Young even lost in huge numbers. He dropped 313 games, more than 300-game winners Grove or Early Wynn *won*.

Young reached the big leagues at 23, in 1890, and pitched until 1911, when he was 44. He was a tall, strong, rural Ohioan who threw hard. He easily had the best control of any pitcher of his era, averaging just 1.49 walks per nine innings over his long career and striking out 2,799. Five times, he won more than 30 games in a season. His career ERA was 2.63. He completed an incredible 751 of his 815 career starts. He pitched three no-hitters, one of them a perfect game. Small wonder that the annual award for the best pitcher in each league is named for him.

Young pitched for five big league teams, beginning with the old Cleveland Spiders, and later the St. Louis Cardinals, Boston Red Sox, Cleveland Indians and Boston Braves. He re-tired in 1911, and in 1937 was elected to the Hall of Fame. He died in 1955.

TWO LIKELY FUTURE HALL-OF-FAMERS

Here are two players who are almost certain to be elected to the Hall of Fame once they've been retired long enough. (Five years is the required time.)

Mike Schmidt

Only seven major league third basemen are in the Hall of Fame. Mike Schmidt will be the eighth. He is quite simply the best third

Phillies third baseman Mike Schmidt.

baseman to ever play the game. One could argue that Brooks Robinson was the better fielder, but not by much. Schmidt won 10 Gold Glove Awards, more than any National Leaguer who has played the position. Certainly, no third baseman has ever hit like him. During his 18-year career (1972 to 1989, all with the Phillies), Schmidt hit 548 home runs, ranking him seventh in history, ahead of Mickey Mantle.

Schmidt was a perfectionist, so intense that his career almost never got off the ground. In 1973, when Schmidt was 23 and in his first full season with the Phillies, he hit .196 and struck out 136 times in just 367 at bats. But once he gained confidence, he was almost unstoppable. Three times, in 1980, 1981 and 1986, he won the National League's Most Valuable Player Award. Eleven times he hit 35 or more home runs, second only to Babe Ruth. He won eight home run championships, a National League record.

He was selected for the All-Star team 12 times. His finest season was 1980, when he led the league with 48 homers and 121 RBIs, and was the MVP of both the league and the World Series.

Schmidt retired in midseason in 1989 when he was 39. He will be eligible for the Hall of Fame in 1994.

Tom Seaver

The New York Mets had lost 95 or more games in every season of their five-year existence. Then, Tom Seaver joined them in 1967, at age 22. Two years later, the laughing-stock Mets won the pennant and the World Series.

Seaver was smart and very competitive, a throwback to the best pitchers of the 1920s. In an era when starting pitchers were frequently satisfied with seven innings of work, Seaver pitched complete games. And not only complete games, but shutouts—61 of them, the seventh-most in history.

Seaver pitched for 20 years and finished his career with a record of 311–205 and an ERA of 2.86. For most of his career, he overpowered hitters with a blazing fastball. His 3,640 strikeouts rank third in history.

Seaver won the Cy Young Award in 1969, when he went 25–7, and again in 1973 and 1975. Three times he led the National League in ERA, and five times he led the league in strikeouts.

The Mets traded Seaver to the Reds in 1977. He returned to the Mets for the 1983 season. He then pitched for the White Sox before ending his career with the Red Sox in 1986. He will be eligible for the Hall of Fame in 1991.

CHAPTER 7

THE GREATEST TEAMS OF ALL TIME

If you are a San Francisco Giants fan, you probably like the Oakland A's about as much as Superman likes kryptonite. Look what you have to put up with: The A's routed your team in the 1989 World Series. The newspapers are full of stories about the A's Jose Canseco and Rickey Henderson. And the A's highlights always come before news of the Giants on TV.

In fact, how can anyone outside of Oakland really *like* the A's? How can anybody in Baltimore or New York or Kansas City or Detroit watch the A's pound their club for an entire summer, and then turn around and root for them in the World Series?

You can't. It's as simple as that. But some teams, like Oakland, are so good, you have to admire them. You grow to respect them. You find that as a true baseball fan, a great team will win you over. Because the truth is that we all want to see baseball played the way it was meant to be played—with power and confidence and excitement and swagger. Watching the A's in the World Series, we think: I hope someday my team can play this way.

Here are seven teams that did.

THE 1907 CHICAGO CUBS

It takes most Cub teams the better part of two years to win 107 games. But in the years

between 1906 and 1908, before they had become lovable losers, the Cubs assembled one of the greatest winning machines in baseball history. In 1906, they won a record 116 games, but were upset in the World Series by their crosstown rivals, the Chicago White Sox. For the next two years, the Cubs won it all. And as we all know, they haven't won a championship since.

The 1907 Cubs finished with a 107–45 record, 17 games ahead of the Pittsburgh Pirates, their nearest competitors. The team was led by the most famous double play combination in history, Hall of Famers Joe Tinker, the shortstop, second baseman Johnny Evers and first baseman/manager Frank Chance. Their ace pitcher, Mordecai "Three Finger" Brown, won 20 or more games six years in a row, and his 2.06 lifetime ERA is the third lowest in history. He, too, is in the Hall of Fame.

The 1907 club was a very unCub-like team. It had no power hitters to take advantage of Wrigley Field's small dimensions, no RBI leaders who smacked the ball up the alleys. Evers and rightfielder Frank "Wildfire" Schulte led the team in home runs, with two apiece. Third baseman Harry Steinfeldt was the club RBI leader, with 70. Only Chance hit as high as .290.

Instead, this team won with superior defense and pitching. The Cubs allowed just 370 runs, 106 fewer than the next best team. Chance, Steinfeldt and catcher Johnny Kling

LIFE

5¢

DEVOTED TO

BASE BALL, TRAP SHOOTING AND GENERAL SPORTS.

Volume 48—No. 7.   Philadelphia, October 27, 1906.   Price, Five Cents.

The 1907 Chicago Cubs finished the year with a 107-45 record.

had the highest fielding averages at their positions in the league. Together, the Cubs committed the fewest errors and scored the highest fielding percentage of any club in the National League.

Even more remarkable than their fielding skill was their pitching. The starting five pitchers were nearly unhittable. All had ERAs of 1.70 or lower. The Cubs' *team* ERA was 1.73. Jack Pfiester (15–9) led the league with a 1.15 ERA, and Carl Lundgren (18–7) was second with an ERA of 1.17. Orval Overall (1.70 ERA) was runner–up in the league in wins, behind Christy Mathewson, with 23. Brown (1.39 ERA) finished with a 20–6 record. Ed Reulbach (1.69 ERA) led the league in winning percentage, with a record of 17–4.

The Cubs faced the Detroit Tigers in the World Series, who boasted Hall of Famers Ty Cobb and Sam Crawford. The first game ended in a 12-inning, 3–3 tie. The Cubs swept the next four games, thanks to great pitching, winning by scores of 3–1, 5–1, 6–1 and 2–0.

THE 1927 NEW YORK YANKEES

These guys could hit. Oh, could they hit. There is a reason why New York's starting lineup was known as Murderers' Row. The 1927 Yankees' *team* batting average was .307. They scored 975 runs. By comparison, the 1989 world champion Oakland A's, with Jose Canseco, Mark McGwire, Dave Henderson and Dave Parker, scored 712. It is a small wonder then that the Yankees finished the season 110–44 and swept the World Series from the Pittsburgh Pirates.

The 1927 Yankees were perhaps the greatest team in the history of baseball. "I would rather pitch a double header against any other club than one game against the Yanks," said St. Louis Browns pitcher Milton Gaston, after losing to them that summer at Yankee Sta-

The 1927 New York Yankees.

The 1929 Philadelphia A's.

dium. "I was so tired when I got through pitching to them the other day that I could hardly drag myself to the hotel."

Who could blame him? The 1927 Yankees roster boasted Hall of Famers Babe Ruth, Lou Gehrig, and centerfielder Earle Combs (.325 lifetime average). Ruth reached his greatest glory in 1927, hitting 60 home runs. Right behind him in the lineup was first baseman Gehrig with 47. Gehrig also knocked in a league-leading 175 runs, while Ruth drove in 164, leftfielder Bob Meusel chipped in 103 and second baseman Tony Lazzeri drove home 102. Combs led the league in hits, with 231. Opposing pitchers, understandably terrified, walked Ruth 138 times, and Gehrig 109 times.

The team's hitting was so astounding it's hard to believe that New York also had one of baseball's all-time best pitching staffs. Hall of Famer Waite Hoyt tied for the league in wins with Chicago's Ted Lyons that year, finishing 22–7, with a league-leading 2.63 ERA. Fellow Hall of Famer Herb Pennock went 19–8. Rookie hurler Wilcy Moore was 19–7 with a 2.28 ERA. Veteran Urban Shocker went 18–6 with a 2.84 ERA. The staff led the league with 11 shutouts, the fewest walks, and a 3.20 ERA.

The Philadelphia A's, with Hall of Famers Ty Cobb, Al Simmons, Mickey Cochrane, Jimmie Foxx and Lefty Grove, were the Yankees' nearest competitors that year and the A's finished 19 games out. In the World Series, the Pirates never had a chance. The day before the Series was to begin, the two teams took batting practice in Pittsburgh's Forbes Field. The Yankees put on a ferocious hitting exhibition while the Pirates watched in disbelief from the stands. Ruth and Gehrig boomed home run after home run over the rightfield fence. Meusel and Lazzeri gave the leftfield seats a similar workout. Afterward, 150-pound Pirates centerfielder Lloyd Waner turned to his brother and the team's right-fielder, Paul Waner. "Gee, they're big guys," he said. "Do they always hit like that?" Pittsburgh seemed to lose heart after the power-hitting display. The Pirates scored just 10 runs in their four straight losses to the Yankees, while Murderers' Row scored 23.

THE 1929 PHILADELPHIA ATHLETICS

In 1927, the Philadelphia A's boasted five Hall of Famers and still couldn't beat the Yankees. Imagine how talented the 1929 A's had to be to capture the pennant from New York by 18 games! They dominated baseball over the next three years, winning two World Series championships and a pennant.

The A's first baseman was "Double X," Jimmie Foxx, who hit 534 career home runs and batted a lifetime .325. The leftfielder was Al Simmons, who hit 307 homers and batted .334. Catcher Mickey Cochrane, a career .320 hitter, was considered the finest receiver of his time. The A's pitching staff was anchored by Lefty Grove (300–141 career record), who is thought to be the greatest lefthanded pitcher in history. All four of these teammates are in the Hall of Fame.

The A's finished with a remarkable record of 104–46 in 1929. It is easy to point to Foxx, Simmons, and Cochrane and claim that the A's won because of their great hitting. Simmons led the league with 157 RBIs, finished second in batting (.365), and was third in home runs with 34. Foxx added 33 homers, 117 RBIs and hit .354. Cochrane and right-fielder Bing Miller each batted over .330 and knocked in over 90 runs. In truth, though, this was an almost perfectly balanced team.

The A's were the best defensive club in the league. They made the fewest errors and had the highest fielding average, and allowed only 615 total runs over the season, 98 fewer than the second best club in the American League.

The A's also had the best pitching. Grove went 20–6, with a league-leading 2.81 ERA. He also topped the league in strikeouts, with 170. George Earnshaw went 24–8 and led the league in wins. The number three starter, Rube Walberg, went 18–11, and fourth man Ed Rommel finished 12–2.

That October, the A's beat the Chicago Cubs in one of the most thrilling World Series finishes of all time. Trailing the Cubs 8–0, going into the bottom of the seventh inning of Game 4, the A's staged an incredible 10-run rally and hung on to win, 10–8. It put the A's ahead in the Series, three games to one. They captured the fifth and final game just as dramatically when, trailing 2–0 in the bottom of the ninth, centerfielder Mule Haas cracked a game-tying two-run home run, and then Simmons and Miller doubled to win the game.

THE 1953 NEW YORK YANKEES

This was a special team, the fifth straight Yankees team to win the World Series, a feat unmatched in the history of baseball.

The Yankees' Murderers' Row team, led by Babe Ruth, never won more than two World Series in a row. The great Bronx Bomber clubs of the 1930s that featured Lou Gehrig and Joe

The 1953 New York Yankees.

The 1961 New York Yankees.

DiMaggio won four consecutive championships. But this club, led by Hall of Famers Mickey Mantle, Yogi Berra and the great lefthanded pitcher, Whitey Ford, won the Series every year from 1949 through 1953.

Mantle was perhaps the greatest player of his day. He was a switch-hitting, fearsome slugger (536 career home runs) who was one of the fastest players of his era. Berra, three times the American League's Most Valuable Player, was the game's finest catcher. Ford's career record was 236–106—a .690 winning percentage, the third highest in history.

That year, seven New Yorkers—Mantle, Berra, rightfielder Hank Bauer, first baseman Johnny Mize, shortstop Phil Rizzuto, and pitchers Allie Reynolds and Johnny Sain— were selected to the 1953 American League All-Star team.

The Yanks won the pennant without much challenge, finishing 99-52 to beat the second-place Cleveland Indians by 8½ games. They scored the most runs, allowed the fewest, led the league in batting and slugging percentage, hurled the most shutouts and compiled the lowest team ERA. Seven of the eight starters hit 10 or more home runs, led by Berra with

27 and Mantle with 21. Ford went 18–6, Sain was 14–7, Vic Raschi was 13–6, and Ed Lopat went 16–4 and topped the league with a 2.42 ERA.

For the third time in five years, the Yankees played the Brooklyn Dodgers in the World Series. The Yankees won the first two games, the Dodgers took the next two, and then the Yanks rallied to win the final two games. Billy Martin, New York's second baseman, won the last game with a single up the middle in the bottom of the ninth.

THE 1961 NEW YORK YANKEES

Do you like home runs? If so, you would have *loved* this team. They hit a record 240. Yes, this was the year that rightfielder Roger Maris smashed 61 homers and Mickey Mantle, who batted right behind Maris in the lineup, clubbed 54—the greatest one-two wallop in the history of the game. Maris led the league with 142 RBIs, and Mantle was fifth with 128.

The Greatest Teams of All Time 81

The 1974 Oakland A's.

But the M&M boys, as Maris and Mantle were known, weren't the whole story. Four other Yankees topped 20 homers that year—first baseman Bill "Moose" Skowron, who had 28; leftfielder Yogi Berra, who smacked 22; and catcher Elston Howard and utility man Johnny Blanchard, who hit 21 each. The Yankees' starting lineup *averaged* 26 home runs apiece.

New York's pitching was just good enough. Ford had his greatest year, going 25–4. And, for that one season, Luis Arroyo was the best reliever in baseball. He went 15–5, with 29 saves. Ralph Terry, who now plays on the Seniors P.G.A. golf tour, went 16–3. The pitchers needed to be good, because all season Detroit was right on New York's tail. The Tigers had a one-two punch of their own—first baseman Norm Cash (.361, 41 HR, 132 RBIs) and leftfielder Rocky Colavito (.290, 45 HR, 140 RBIs). The Tigers finished 101–61. The Yankees ended the season 109–53, and then beat Cincinnati in the World Series, four games to one.

THE 1974 OAKLAND A'S

The 1949–1953 Yankees won the World Series five straight times, and the 1936–1939 Yankees won the championship four times in a row. The next best record belongs to the Mustache Gang, the 1972–1974 Oakland A's.

The A's were unlike any other baseball team, a colorful group, to say the least. At the urging of team owner Charles Finley, they all grew glorious mustaches at a time when ballplayers were expected to be clean shaven. The players were underpaid and argued with Finley constantly. But mostly, they bickered among themselves. Reggie Jackson tussled with centerfielder Bill North. Catcher Dave Duncan, now Oakland's pitching coach, fought with third baseman Sal Bando. Relief pitcher Rollie Fingers fought with starting pitcher Blue Moon Odom, and Odom fought with fellow starter Vida Blue.

On the field, though, the A's personality clashes didn't seem to matter. They won for a lot of good reasons: because Bert Campaneris was among the best shortstops of his era; because Joe Rudi was a great clutch hitter and leftfielder; because Bando provided strong hitting and quiet leadership; because Fingers, Blue, Ken Holtzman and Catfish Hunter anchored the best pitching staff in baseball; and because of Reggie Jackson's enormous home runs.

The 1974 A's finished 90–72 in the American League West, 6 games ahead of the second-place Texas Rangers. They allowed just 551 runs over the season, 106 less than the next best team in their division. They also had the most stolen bases and the lowest ERA in the league. Six Oakland players—Jackson, Bando, Hunter, Fingers, Campaneris and Rudi—were selected to the 1974 All-Star team. Jackson, Rudi, Bando and catcher Gene Tenace each hit more than 20 home runs.

North led the league with 54 stolen bases. Hunter went 25–12 with a 2.49 ERA, and won the Cy Young Award.

The A's steamrollered the Baltimore Orioles three games to one in the league playoffs, and then disposed of the National League champion Los Angeles Dodgers four games to one in the World Series. The A's might have won even more championships had they stuck together a few more years. But their constant battles with Finley wore them out, and most of the stars left the team by 1977, as soon as they qualified for free agency.

THE 1976 CINCINNATI REDS

The 1976 Reds, known everywhere as the Big Red Machine, had such an outstanding lineup that seven of the club's eight regulars were chosen for the All-Star game that sum-

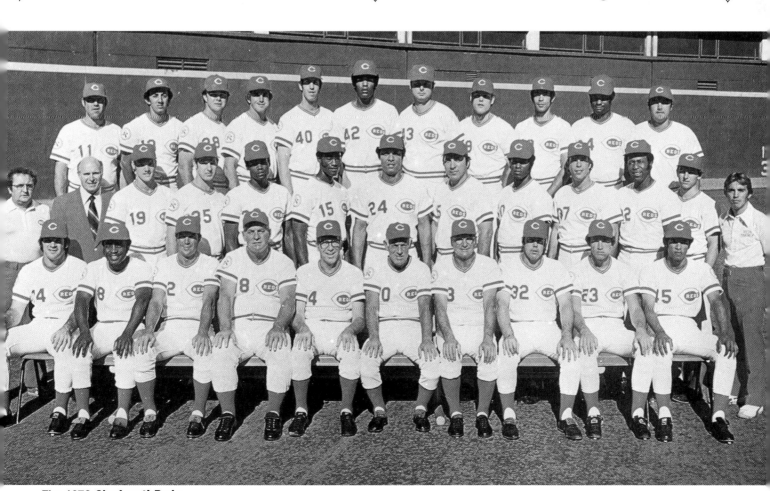

The 1976 Cincinnati Reds.

mer. Centerfielder Cesar Geronimo was the only Reds starter bypassed, and he finished the season batting .307. From 1970 to 1977, four different Reds—catcher Johnny Bench, second baseman Joe Morgan, leftfielder George Foster and leftfielder Pete Rose—won the National League MVP Award (a team total of six times). Bench was a wizard both behind and at the plate, one of the greatest ever at his position. Ditto for Morgan, who was a brilliant fielder, a daring base thief and a feared power hitter. Both Bench and Morgan have already been elected to the Hall of Fame.

First baseman Tony Perez will certainly be a candidate for the Hall of Fame. In the 10 seasons from 1967 to 1976, the big Cuban averaged 26 home runs and 103 RBIs a year, and made six All-Star squads. Third baseman Pete Rose was simply the most persistent hitter in history. He holds the record for hits, with 4,256. Shortstop Dave Concepcion was the premier shortstop of the 1970s, winning five Gold Gloves for being the best at his position. Rightfielder Ken Griffey may be better known today as the father of Seattle Mariners star Ken Griffey, Jr., but he was a three-time All-Star with Sparky Anderson's Reds. These were the engines that drove the Big Red Machine.

And drive it they did. In 1976, Foster hammered 29 home runs and knocked in 121 runs. Morgan, the Most Valuable Player that year, hit 27 homers, drove in 111, scored 113, walked 114 times and swiped 60 bases. Rose led the league with 130 runs scored and 215 hits. Five Reds hit over .300—Griffey (.336), Rose (.323), Morgan (.320), Geronimo (.307) and Foster (.306).

This team needed to hit well because the Reds pitchers weren't nearly as good as the hitters. Gary Nolan had real talent but was troubled throughout his career by arm injuries. The rest—Jack Billingham, Fred Norman and Pat Zachry—were decent pitchers who were fortunate to pitch for a team loaded with offensive talent. Nolan, the staff's top winner, finished 15–9. Zachry won 14. Norman and Billingham won 12 games each. Stopper Rawley Eastwick provided a league-leading 26 saves.

According to an old baseball saying, good pitching will beat good hitting. But not when the hitting is *this* good. The Reds won the National League West by 10 games, with a 102–60 mark. They shut out Philadelphia three games to none in the playoffs. In the World Series, they swept the Yankees, four games to none.

NATIONAL LEAGUE EAST

Chicago Cubs Important Dates:

1876—Charter member of the National League.

1902—Cubs officially adopted as the team name. They were previously known as the White Stockings, the Colts and the Orphans.

1916—Wrigley Field opens.

1930—Hack Wilson drives in a record 190 runs.

1935—The Cubs win a record 21 games in a row on their way to the 1935 pennant.

1945—The Cubs' most recent trip to the World Series. They lose to Detroit, four games to three.

1958—Ernie Banks becomes the first member of a team with a losing record to win the MVP Award.

1960—Don Cardwell throws a no-hitter in his first Cubs appearance.

1961—The Cubs decide not to hire a manager, and instead appoint a "college of coaches" to run the team.

1981—The Wrigley family sells the Cubs to the Tribune Company.

1988—First night game at Wrigley Field.

The last time the Cubs won the World Series was 1908. Fans in other cities must wonder how Cubs fans can stay so crazy about their team. They'd understand if they ever walked into the beloved Wrigley Field.

They'd see the green ivy lining the outfield walls, and the cozy diamond with seats so close to the playing field you can shout to the players and know that they'll hear you. They'd see the ancient, hand-operated centerfield scoreboard, and the crazy fans known as the Bleacher Bums who sit beneath it.

Some of the game's greatest players have worn Cubbie blue. There were Joe Tinker, Johnny Evers and Frank Chance, the most famous double play combination in baseball history. And Hall of Fame catcher Gabby Hartnett, who helped the Cubs win the 1935 pennant. There was leftfielder Hack Wilson, who drove in a record 190 runs in 1930. And Hall of Fame shortstop Ernie Banks, known as Mr. Cub, and the best-loved Cub of all. Banks, who hit 512 career homers, played for the

Cubs for his entire 19-year career, and never once played on a pennant-winning team.

The closest he came was in 1969, when the Cubs, led by Banks, manager Leo Durocher, Hall of Fame leftfielder Billy Williams, Cooperstown candidates third baseman Ron Santo and pitcher Ferguson Jenkins, fell to the Mets in September after leading the National League East all summer.

Cubs fans still haven't gotten over that loss. Perhaps the current batch of Cubs stars—second baseman Ryne Sandberg, rightfielder Andre Dawson, first baseman Mark Grace and pitcher Greg Maddux—will finally lead them to that long dreamed-of championship. As Cubs fans are known to say at the start of every season, maybe this will be the year.

Montreal Expos
Important Dates:

1969—Montreal Expos join the National League.
1969—Claude Raymond is the first Canadian to play for the Expos. Other Canadians will include Bill Atkinson, Larry Landreth and Doug Frobel.
1977—Olympic Stadium opens.
1979—First Expos team to finish over .500.
1981—Tim Raines wins the first of his five stolen base titles.
1981—The Expos reach the league playoffs for the first time in the club's history.

The Expos' first hero was redheaded rightfielder Rusty Staub, known in Montreal as "Le Grand Orange." In Montreal, where both French and English are spoken, batters are called *frappeurs*; pitchers are known as *lancers*. When the Expos joined the National League in 1969, they transformed baseball into a truly international sport.

Like every expansion team, the Expos suffered through some bleak years until their farm system had a chance to develop a crop of talented players. By the time their new stadium opened in 1977, the Expos had a roster that featured some of the game's greatest stars, including outfielders Andre Dawson and Tim Raines, and catcher Gary Carter—all likely to be candidates for the Hall of Fame.

The Expos still haven't won a division title or played in a World Series. But they came close twice. They missed out the first time because they didn't take a chance. They missed out the second time because they did.

In 1981—the year the baseball season was split by a players' strike—Montreal won a piece of the National League East title. The Expos seemed ready to dominate the division. They had Dawson, Carter and Raines in the lineup, and Steve Rogers on the mound. All they needed was a decent second baseman and some proven bench players. But they traded for neither.

In 1989, they seemed poised again to win their division. This time, the Expos traded three of their top minor league pitching prospects for lefthander Mark Langston. Disaster struck when the Expos slumped and finished fourth and then Langston and two other starters, Pascual Perez and Bryn Smith, filed for free agency and signed with other teams.

In the 1990s, the Expos have had to completely rebuild their pitching staff. They learned the hard way that trading is risky business.

New York Mets
Important Dates:

1962—Mets join the National League. Casey Stengel is hired as manager.

1962—Mets lose their first nine games and finish 40–120.
1964—Mets move from the Polo Grounds to Shea Stadium. Naturally, they lose their first game there.
1965—Stengel retires.
1966—Mets escape cellar for the first time, finishing ninth.
1967—Tom Seaver joins the team.
1969—The "Miracle Mets" win the World Series.
1984—Dwight Gooden joins the team.
1989—Mets win 90 or more games for the sixth year in a row.

They began in 1962 as the Amazin' Mets, a collection of lovable has-beens and hopefuls who captured the hearts of all those New Yorkers who never could warm up to the Yankees. The Mets first baseman was Marvelous Marv Throneberry, possibly the worst fielding first baseman in the history of the game. Roger Craig, now the San Francisco Giants manager, was the Mets pitching ace and he lost 24 games. The 1962 team finished 40–120, 60½ games out of first place.

In 1969, they became the Miracle Mets, a team of young, enthusiastic, no-name players who unexpectedly won the World Series after finishing in ninth place the year before. Their pitching staff, nearly anonymous when the season began, included Tom Seaver, Nolan Ryan, Jerry Koosman and Tug McGraw. Their young shortstop was Bud Harrelson, who now manages the Mets. That year, the Mets beat the heavily favored Cubs for the National League East title, and then stunned the baseball world by upsetting the Baltimore Orioles, led by Jim Palmer, Frank Robinson and Brooks Robinson, four games to one in the World Series.

Since 1986, they've been the Awesome Mets, a team loaded with hitters and blessed with one of the finest pitching staffs in history. They have been led on the field by first baseman Keith Hernandez, catcher Gary Carter and rightfielder Darryl Strawberry, all potential Hall of Famers, and on the mound by Dwight Gooden, Ron Darling and Bob Ojeda. In 1989, they dominated the National League, finishing 108–54, 21½ games ahead of their nearest competitor. The Mets have been the pennant favorites every year since.

Philadelphia Phillies Important Dates:

1876—Charter member of the National League, but they drop out during the season.
1883—Club returns to the National League.
1903—Leftfield bleachers in Philadelphia Park collapse, killing 12 and injuring 232.
1915—Phillies win the pennant, their last until 1950.
1916—Grover Alexander pitches a record 16 shutouts.
1919—Phillies lose to the Giants, 6–1, in 51 minutes, the fastest game in history.
1935—Phillies lose baseball's first night game to the Reds in Cincinnati.
1938—Phillies move to Shibe Park.
1944—Team name temporarily changed to Blue Jays.
1961—Phillies lose a record 23 consecutive games.
1964—Jim Bunning pitches the franchise's first perfect game.
1971—Veterans Stadium opens.
1972—Phillies acquire Steve Carlton, who wins 27 games that year.
1980—Phillies win their first world championship.

The Phillies fans are the loudest in baseball, and by far the most critical. If you wonder why they often boo their own players, consider this: The Phils joined the National League as a charter member in 1876, and went 104 years before winning a world championship.

But the truth is the Phillies have fielded some of the greatest players and most exciting teams in baseball history. Pitchers Grover Cleveland Alexander (373 wins) and Robin

Roberts (286 wins), both Hall of Famers, wore Phillies red. So did Jim Bunning (224 wins), the only pitcher besides Nolan Ryan to hurl a no-hitter in each league. Rightfielder Chuck Klein, the 1933 Triple Crown winner and Hall of Famer, was a Phillie. So were Hall of Famer Steve Carlton (329 wins) and third baseman Mike Schmidt (548 home runs), who is certain to win election to the Hall of Fame.

The Phillies teams of the early 1980s were strong, winning the World Series in 1980 and the National League pennant in 1983. When stars such as Schmidt retired and Pete Rose, Joe Morgan, Steve Carlton and Manny Trillo left in the mid-80s, the team slumped. But a slew of new faces gives Phillies fans great cause for hope in the 1990s.

The Pirates Roberto Clemente.

Pittsburgh Pirates
Important Dates:

1887—The Pittsburgh Alleghenies join the National League.
1891—Name changed to Pirates.
1900—Louisville drops out of the National League, sells Hall of Famers Honus Wagner, Fred Clarke and Rube Waddell to the Pirates.
1903—Pirates win the pennant for the third consecutive year. They lose the first World Series to the Red Sox.
1909—Forbes Field opens; Pirates win 110 games and the World Series.
1960—Bill Mazeroski homers in the ninth inning of the seventh game of the World Series, to win the championship from the Yankees.
1970—Three Rivers Stadium opens.

When you think of the Pirates of the 1970s, you think of Hall of Fame first baseman Willie Stargell swinging his huge bat like Paul Bunyan, rightfielder Dave "The Cobra" Parker lashing hits against and over the outfield walls, catcher Manny Sanguillen whacking bad pitches for doubles like Yogi Berra once did, and John "The Candy Man" Candelaria blowing strikes by everybody.

The Pirates had a swagger and an attitude that carried them to six division titles, two pennants and two world championships during the 1970s. Their leader was one of the franchise's greatest players, the incomparable Roberto Clemente. The Hall of Fame rightfielder won four batting titles, batted a lifetime .317 and collected 3,000 hits before he died in an airplane crash after the 1972 season.

As great as Clemente was, he was not the Pirates all time finest player. That honor goes to Hall of Fame shortstop Honus Wagner, who had 3,430 hits, stole 722 bases and batted .329 over a 21-year career that lasted until 1917. Ten years later, the Pirates fielded a team with three other Hall of Famers—third baseman Pie Traynor, rightfielder Paul "Big Poison" Waner and his brother, leftfielder Lloyd "Little Poison" Waner.

In the tradition of the great Pirates before them, current stars like outfielders Bobby Bonilla and Barry Bonds seem ready to carry the Bucs to their next championship.

St. Louis Cardinals
Important Dates:

1876—The St. Louis Brown Stockings become a charter member of the National League.
1877—Team withdraws from the National League.
1892—St. Louis rejoins the National League.
1900—Cardinals becomes the official team name.
1924—Rogers Hornsby hits a record .424.
1966—Busch Stadium opens.
1968—Bob Gibson pitches 13 shutouts on his way to a 1.12 ERA, a National League record.
1979—Lou Brock retires with a record 938 stolen bases.

In 1919, two years after he began his 25-year career as president of the Cardinals, Branch Rickey invented the farm system. Rather than compete in a bidding war with wealthier clubs for top prospects on independent minor league teams, Rickey decided to operate his own farm clubs and develop his own talent. These farm teams were like training schools for the Cardinals, and the best of the farm players were "promoted" to St. Louis. This system worked so well that soon other major league teams started using it.

Rickey's first homegrown players included leftfielder Chick Hafey and first baseman Jim Bottomley, both Hall of Famers. Before long, pitcher Dizzy Dean, leftfielder Joe Medwick and third baseman Pepper Martin, the stars of the 1934 "Gashouse Gang" championship team, came of age. Later, stars such as rightfielder Stan Musial, shortstop Marty Marion and pitcher Bob Gibson came up the ranks.

The farm system has kept the Cardinals competitive for years. Their championship teams of the 1960s were built around Bob Gibson, one of the most feared righthanders in the history of the game, and leftfielder Lou Brock, one of the greatest base stealers ever, along with Rickey Henderson. The pennant-winning Cardinal teams of the 1980s revolved around shortstop Ozzie Smith, centerfielder Willie McGee and pitcher John Tudor.

The baseball world is waiting to see who comes off the St. Louis farm in the 1990s.

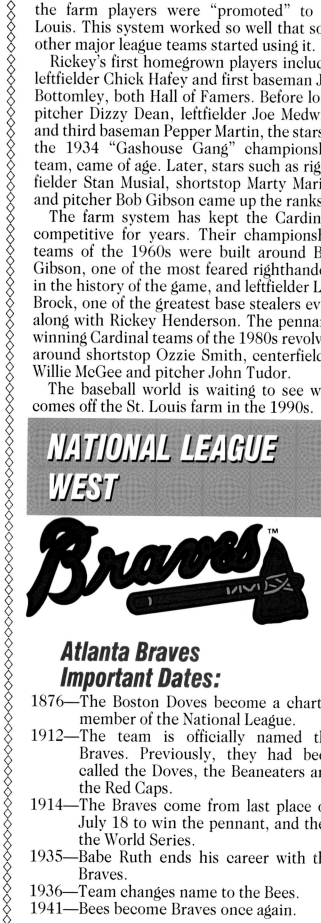

NATIONAL LEAGUE WEST

Atlanta Braves
Important Dates:

1876—The Boston Doves become a charter member of the National League.
1912—The team is officially named the Braves. Previously, they had been called the Doves, the Beaneaters and the Red Caps.
1914—The Braves come from last place on July 18 to win the pennant, and then the World Series.
1935—Babe Ruth ends his career with the Braves.
1936—Team changes name to the Bees.
1941—Bees become Braves once again.

1948—Braves win the pennant behind pitchers Warren Spahn and Johnny Sain, but lose to Cleveland in the World Series.
1953—Braves move to Milwaukee.
1957–
1958—Braves win two straight pennants and the 1957 World Series.
1966—Braves move to Atlanta.
1974—Hank Aaron hits his 715th home run to break Babe Ruth's career record.
1977—Owner Ted Turner appoints himself manager during a 17-game losing streak. He loses to Pittsburgh, 2–1, then returns to the front office.
1982–
1983—Dale Murphy wins the MVP Award two consecutive years.

There was a time when the Braves were as powerful as Cincinnati's famous Big Red Machine and drew more than two million fans a year. But that was back in the 1950s when they were known as the Milwaukee Braves.

The Braves rightfielder then was the all-time home run king, Hank Aaron, and their lineup featured three other future Hall of Famers—third baseman Eddie Mathews, second baseman Red Schoendienst and pitcher Warren Spahn, the winningest lefthander in history (363 wins). The Braves won the World Series in 1957, the pennant in 1958, and lost the pennant in a playoff in 1959. But when the team stopped winning pennants, the fans lost interest, and in 1966, the team moved. Again.

You need a scorecard and a roadmap to keep track of this franchise. From 1876 to 1952 they played in Boston. They played the next 13 seasons in Milwaukee before settling in Atlanta.

The Milwaukee years were certainly the best in the club's history. The Boston period, on the other hand, was especially grim. Twenty-nine seasons between 1901 and 1952, the team finished 30 or more games out of first place. One of those seasons was 1913, when the team finished 69–82, 31½ games out of first. The very next year, led by Hall of Fame shortstop Rabbit Maranville, the Miracle Braves rallied like the Miracle Mets and won the World Series. Since moving to Atlanta, the Braves have won two division titles, but more often than not have finished near the bottom of the pack. Entering the 1990s, though, there is reason for hope. The club is brimming with some of the most outstanding young pitchers in baseball. Things are looking so good that the Braves, the nomads of the National League, may even stay in Atlanta for a while.

Cincinnati Reds
Important Dates:

1876—Cincinnati Red Stockings become a charter member of the National League.

1881—Cincinnati drops out of the National League because the league would not permit beer sales in the ballpark.

1890—Club rejoins the National League.

1919—Cincinnati defeats the Chicago White Sox to win the World Series.

1935—Reds win baseball's first night game which is played at Crosley Field.

1939–
1940—Reds win back-to-back pennants, and the 1940 World Series.

1970—Riverfront Stadium opens.

1976—Reds win their fourth pennant and second world championship of the decade.

1978—Pete Rose compiles a 44-game hitting streak.

1985—Rose gets his 4,192nd hit, breaking Ty Cobb's career record.

Ask a Cincinnatian about baseball, and he will tell you about the Big Red Machine, the powerful Cincinnati ball team of the 1970s. He'll talk about Hall of Fame second baseman Joe Morgan, twice the league's Most Valuable Player, and one of the greatest clutch hitters and base runners in the history of the game. He'll mention Hall of Fame catcher Johnny Bench, who also won two Most Valuable Player Awards, and was perhaps the best to ever play his position. He'll go on and on about Pete Rose, the man who broke Ty Cobb's career hits record. He'll describe leftfielder George Foster's monstrous homers, first baseman Tony Perez's power hitting and Dave Concepcion's wizardry at shortstop. The Big Red Machine won two world championships, two pennants and one division title in seven years, a streak surpassed only by the New York Yankees of the 1950s.

The Reds had been saving up for that streak for a long, long time. They were one of the founding members of the National League, having joined in 1876, and for most of their history they were among the game's weaker teams.

The Reds won the 1919 World Series—but probably because eight members of the notorious Chicago "Black Sox" lost it on purpose.

They flourished briefly again from 1939 to 1940 when pitchers Bucky Walters and Paul Derringer led them first to a pennant and then a world championship, but then finished under .500 from 1945 to 1956.

In 1960 they made a series of marvelous trades for pitching and hitting, and won the pennant, but didn't win again until 1970, when Sparky Anderson took over as manager of the team and led it through its glory years.

Now the Reds seem poised to triumph again. With centerfielder Eric Davis and All–Star shortstop Barry Larkin leading the offense, and the "Nasty Boys," as the relief pitchers have named themselves, nailing down games from the bullpen, they look like the Big Red Machine all over again.

Houston Astros
Important Dates:

1962—Houston Colt 45s join the National League.

1965—Astrodome opens and the team changes its name to the Astros.

1967—Don Wilson pitches the first Astro no-hitter.

1969—Larry Dierker is the club's first 20-game winner.

1972—Astros finish above .500 for the first time.

1979—Pitcher J.R. Richard strikes out 313 batters.

1980—Houston wins its first National League West title.

1986—Houston wins its second National League West title.

As good as the Mets were in 1986—and their 108–54 record was incredibly good—the Astros nearly beat them that year in the National League playoffs. Led by Nolan Ryan, Mike Scott and leftfielder Jose Cruz, the Astros tied the series at two games apiece, before losing Game 5 in 12 innings and Game 6 in the 16th inning.

But even that series paled in comparison to Houston's 1980 battle against Philadelphia in the National League playoffs. Every game except the first went into extra innings, with the Phillies winning the deciding game by scoring the tie-breaker in the 10th.

Houston's good years came after a long dry spell. In fact, they finished with more wins than losses just once in their first 17 years, after joining the National League in 1962. It seemed to take the Astros years to figure out that big, lumbering sluggers are not well-suited to the Astrodome. Long fly balls tend to die in the heavy air of the enclosed ballpark. In the last few years, they have concentrated on signing quick, aggressive players, and seem ready to climb into pennant contention again.

Los Angeles Dodgers Important Dates:

1890—The Brooklyn Superbas jump from the American Association to the National League.

1916—Dodgers win their first modern era pennant.

1947—Jackie Robinson becomes the first black player to join the major leagues.

1951—Dodgers lose pennant playoff to the Giants on Bobby Thomson's home run.

1955—Dodgers beat the Yankees in the World Series for the first time in six tries. It is their first Series win.

1958—Dodgers move to Los Angeles.

1962—Dodger Stadium opens.

1965—Sandy Koufax pitches a perfect game against Chicago. It is his fourth no-hitter.

1988—Orel Hershiser hurls a record 59 consecutive scoreless innings. Dodgers beat Oakland in the World Series.

Of all the teams in history, few were as appealing as the Brooklyn Dodgers of the 1950s. America followed them like the afternoon soap operas. There was Jackie Robinson, the tough, courageous second baseman who was the first black man to break into the major leagues. Behind the plate was Roy Campanella, three times the league's Most Valuable Player, and among the best ever at his position. Duke Snider, the supremely talented slugger, patrolled centerfield. At shortstop was team captain Pee Wee Reese, who anchored the infield. All four are in the Hall of Fame. The great Gil Hodges played first, and Carl Erskine, who threw two no-hitters, ruled on the mound.

But for all their talent, they could never beat the rival New York Yankees in the World Series. Every year it was, "Wait till next year." The Dodgers lost to the Yankees in five World Series—in 1941, 1947, 1949, 1952 and 1953—before finally beating them in 1955. When the Yankees won back the title in 1956, the cry in Brooklyn was, "Wait till *last* year."

When the Dodgers moved to Los Angeles in 1958, they also changed their image from runner-up to champion. It took the Brooklyn Dodgers 66 years to win their first World Series but the Los Angeles Dodgers won one in just two years.

The typical Dodgers team changed, too. Brooklyn's Ebbets Field was tiny, so the team was built around sluggers instead of base stealers or pitchers. Dodger Stadium, on the other hand, is spacious. The great Los Angeles teams have been built around pitchers such as Sandy Koufax, Don Drysdale, Don Sutton, Fernando Valenzuela and Orel Hershiser, and base runners such as Maury Wills, Davey Lopes and Steve Sax.

But there is one thing about the Dodger tradition that has not changed. The Dodgers are still arguably the most popular team in baseball—nearly every year, they lead the major leagues in attendance.

San Diego Padres Important Dates:

1969—Padres join the National League.
1975—Randy Jones becomes Padres first 20-game winner.
1978—Padres finish above .500 for the first time.
1980—"Trader Jack" McKeon named general manager.
1982—Padres sign free agent Steve Garvey.
1984—Padres win the National League pennant, lose to the Tigers in the World Series.
1989—Tony Gwynn wins his fourth batting title.

Jack McKeon loves to trade players. Show him an opposing team's roster, and he goes into a feeding frenzy. Like a baseball Dracula, he constantly needs new blood.

"Trader Jack" took over the Padres in 1980, first as general manager, and from 1988 to 1990, also as field manager. He has reshaped the Padres many times.

One day in 1980, he made two trades, dumping five players and getting eight in return. In 1982 alone, he made 13 separate

trades. Some have involved the biggest names in the game. Over the years, Ozzie Smith, Kevin Mitchell, Sandy Alomar, Jr. and Hall of Fame pitchers Gaylord Perry and Rollie Fingers have passed through his hands.

Not all his deals panned out, but enough did to lead the 1984 Padres to a pennant. It was only the second time the team had finished over .500 in its 16-year history.

The best player in the Padres' history, however, did not become a Padre as a result of a trade. Rightfielder Tony Gwynn, four times the National League batting champion, is a product of the San Diego farm system.

San Francisco Giants Important Dates:

1876—New York Mutuals become a charter member of the National League.
1902—John McGraw named manager of the team, now known as the Giants.
1908—Christy Mathewson wins 37 games.
1924—Giants win their fourth pennant in a row, the team's eighth in 14 years.
1930—Bill Terry gets 254 hits, bats .401.
1934—Carl Hubbell strikes out Babe Ruth, Lou Gehrig, Jimmie Foxx, Al Simmons and Joe Cronin consecutively in the All-Star Game.
1947—Mel Ott retires with 511 home runs.
1951—Bobby Thomson hits a ninth-inning home run to beat the Dodgers in a playoff for the National League pennant.
1954—Giants beat Cleveland in the World Series. Centerfielder Willie Mays makes an over-the-shoulder catch of Vic Wertz's 440-foot hit. Dusty Rhodes pinch hits a home run to win the game.
1958—Giants move to San Francisco.

1962—Giants beat Dodgers again in a pennant playoff.

1973—Mays retires with 660 home runs.

1989—Giants win the pennant; Kevin Mitchell hits 47 home runs.

Frequently in their long history, the Giants have had to play in the shadows. In New York, they were often in the shadow of the Yankees. Now, in San Francisco, they play second fiddle to the A's.

Bad timing has had a lot to do with it. As the Giants were winning their third consecutive pennant in 1923, many of their fans were defecting to brand new Yankee Stadium to cheer Babe Ruth. When Willie Mays, their most exciting star, came along in 1951, the Dodgers and Yankees had their own Hall of Fame centerfielders, Duke Snider and Mickey Mantle. Now, Will Clark and Kevin Mitchell have to compete for attention with Jose Canseco, Mark McGwire, Rickey Henderson and Dave Stewart of the A's.

Sometimes the Giants combined bad judgment with bad timing. For years the Giants' farm system produced loads of talented players, more perhaps than any other team in baseball. But more often than not, it seemed just as these players were ready for greatness, the Giants would trade them away. Among the young players who were traded by the Giants and who went on to remarkable careers with other teams were first baseman Orlando Cepeda, pitcher Gaylord Perry, and big-hitting outfielder George Foster.

New general manager Al Rosen has built a championship team. It's just bad luck that across the Bay Bridge is a club that casts a big shadow.

CHAPTER 9

THE TEAMS OF THE AMERICAN LEAGUE

AMERICAN LEAGUE EAST

Baltimore Orioles Important Dates:

1954—St. Louis Browns move to Baltimore, and become the Orioles.

1955—Brooks Robinson joins the Orioles.

1966—Club acquires Frank Robinson, who wins Triple Crown and MVP; O's win the World Series.

1968—Earl Weaver named manager.

1974—Orioles win fifth division title in six years.

1976—Jim Palmer wins second consecutive Cy Young Award.

1983—Orioles win the World Series.

When you think of the Orioles, you think of great pitching. You think of Hall of Famer Jim Palmer and his 268 career wins. You think of Dave McNally and Steve Stone. You think of all those Mikes—Flanagan, Cuellar, Boddicker, Torrez. In the 12 years from 1969 to 1980, the Orioles pitchers won six Cy Young Awards.

Pitching was the cornerstone upon which feisty Earl Weaver, the greatest of all Baltimore managers, built his teams. In 1971, each of his four starters won 20 games or more. Over 17 years, beginning in 1968, he managed 22 20-game winners.

But pitching hasn't been Baltimore's only strength. The Orioles of the 1960s and 1970s also included slugger Frank Robinson (586 career home runs) in rightfield, and Brooks Robinson and Luis Aparicio, two of the greatest fielders ever, at third base and shortstop, respectively. All three are in the Hall of Fame.

Baltimore won its first pennant and World Series in 1966, and finished first or second 14 times in the next 17 years.

The O's success is quite a change from the days before the team moved to Baltimore from St. Louis in 1954. The St. Louis Browns won just one pennant between 1902 and 1953 before moving and finding success in Baltimore. Now, armed with a new batch of talented, young pitchers, the O's appear ready to challenge for the pennant again.

Boston Red Sox Important Dates:

1903—The Red Sox win the first World Series, defeating the Pittsburgh Pirates.

1912—Fenway Park opens.

1920—Boston owner Harry Frazee goes broke, sells Babe Ruth to the Yankees.

1941—Ted Williams bats .406; no one has hit .400 since.

1948—Red Sox lose pennant playoff to Cleveland.

1967—Red Sox lose the World Series to the Cardinals.

1975—Red Sox lose the World Series to the Reds.

1978—Yankee shortstop Bucky Dent hits a home run to beat the Red Sox in a pennant playoff.

1986—Red Sox lose the World Series again, this time to the Mets.

1988—Wade Boggs wins his fourth straight batting title.

Baltimore is known for its great pitchers; Boston, on the other hand, has produced some fabulous leftfielders. From 1939 until 1960, the great Ted Williams (521 career home runs, .344 lifetime average) played in the shadow of the Green Monster, the 37-foot high leftfield wall in Boston's cozy Fenway Park. When he retired, another Hall of Famer, Carl Yastrzemski (452 homers, 3,419 career hits) took his place. And in 1975, when Yaz slowed down and moved to first base, Hall of Fame candidate Jim Rice (382 homers) took over in left.

The Red Sox, in fact, have provided baseball with more than a dozen of its greatest stars. Unfortunately, past owners sold off or traded many of them before they could win the Red Sox a championship. The worst offender was Sox owner Harry Frazee, who sold Babe Ruth and Hall of Fame pitcher Herb Pennock to the rival Yankees so he could finance his Broadway shows. As a result, Boston has not won a World Series since beating the Cubs in 1918.

The Sox have come close, though—agonizingly close. No true Sox fan has ever completely gotten over Boston narrowly losing the 1967 World Series to the Cardinals, the 1975 Series to the Reds, or the 1986 Series to the Mets.

Now the Sox have a new collection of stars, including batting champion Wade Boggs and Cy Young Award winner Roger Clemens. Perhaps this group will at long last win a World Series for Boston.

Cleveland Indians Important Dates:

1901—Cleveland becomes a charter member of the American League.

1915—Team officially named the Indians. Previous names included the Forest Cities, the Spiders, the Blues, the Bronchos and the Naps.

1920—The Indians win the pennant, their last until 1948. Second baseman Bill Wambsganss turns the only unassisted triple play in World Series history.

1920—Cleveland shortstop Ray Chapman is killed by a pitch thrown by Yankee pitcher Carl Mays.

1932—Cleveland Municipal Stadium opens.

1947—Outfielder Larry Doby is the first black player in the American League.

Larry Doby, the first black player in the American League.

1948—Indians win the World Series. Pitcher Bob Feller captures his seventh strike-out title.

1954—Indians win 111 games and the pennant.

1975—Frank Robinson is the first black manager of a major league team.

It is no accident that *Major League,* the hit baseball movie, chose Cleveland as the home of its fictitious, worse-than-terrible baseball team. The real Indians have finished first just three times in 90 years—in 1920, 1948, and most recently, in 1954.

Though they haven't won many titles, Cleveland has often fielded strong teams. From 1948 to 1956, they captured one World Series, one pennant and finished second five times. Only the great Yankees of the 1950s, led by Mickey Mantle, Whitey Ford and Yogi Berra, kept them from winning more.

The Indians were a team of solid hitters (Hall of Fame shortstop Lou Boudreau, slugging centerfielder Larry Doby and power hitting third baseman Al Rosen) and superior pitchers (Hall of Famers Bob Feller, Bob Lemon and Early Wynn, and 20-game winners Herb Score and Mike Garcia). In 1948, the Tribe won a thrilling pennant playoff from the Boston Red Sox, and then beat the Boston Braves, four games to two, in the World Series. In 1954, they won a league record 111 games, before losing the championship to the New York Giants, whose star was Willie Mays.

Cleveland remained a contender until April 17, 1960, when they traded rightfielder Rocky Colavito to Detroit for shortstop Harvey Kuenn. Colavito was the defending American League home run champion. He had hit 83 homers in the previous two years and would end up hitting 374 in his career. The Tribe traded him for the league's best singles hitter. It was like trading in your Cadillac for a VW bug. After that, the Indians seemed to lose their spark and their direction. In the last 30 years, the Indians have finished higher than fourth just once.

But that may be about to change. Today's Indians boast a fine pitching staff—shades of the 1950s—that may carry them back to contention in the American League East.

Detroit Tigers Important Dates:

1895—While playing in the Western League, the franchise takes the name "Tigers."

1901—Tigers become a charter member of the American League.

1907–
1909—Tigers win three consecutive pennants.

1915—Ty Cobb wins ninth consecutive batting title.

1938—Briggs Stadium opens; name changed to Tiger Stadium in 1961.

1938—Hank Greenberg hits 58 home runs.

1968—Denny McLain wins 31 games, the last time a pitcher has won 30 or more.

1984—Tigers beat the Padres in the World Series.

Home movies of the Tigers of 70 years ago would show Ty Cobb slashing a single to center, then stealing second, spikes flying, with Hall of Fame rightfielder Harry Heilmann knocking him home.

In the 1930s, the images would be of Hank Greenberg belting home runs into the upper leftfield deck of sold-out Briggs (now Tiger) Stadium. There was the great Mickey Cochrane behind the plate, and Charlie Gehringer scooping up balls behind second, to lead Detroit to a World Series victory in 1935.

The Tigers of the '60s featured rightfielder Al Kaline smacking homers into the cheap seats, righthander Denny McLain winning 31 games in 1968, and portly Mickey Lolich winning three from the St. Louis Cardinals that October to lead Detroit to victory in the World Series.

The Tigers have a history of having home-grown talent; they have gotten some of their finest players through their farm system. Most of the franchise's all-time greats—the stars of those home movies, including Cobb, Greenberg, Rudy York, Heilmann, Gehringer, Kaline and Lolich—came to the team that way. Modern stars like Alan Trammell, Kirk Gibson, Jack Morris and Lou Whitaker also came out of the farm clubs.

Detroit is one of the oldest and most fabled teams in baseball. It will be exciting to see the new stars the Tigers produce in the 1990s.

Milwaukee Brewers
Important Dates:

1969—Seattle Pilots join the American League.
1970—Franchise moves to Milwaukee, and is renamed the Brewers.
1978—Brewers finish above .500 for the first time.
1982—Brewers win the pennant; Robin Yount voted MVP; Pete Vuckovich wins the Cy Young Award.
1989—Yount wins his second MVP Award.

Nine seasons after the Milwaukee Brewers joined the American League (they began life in 1969 as the Seattle Pilots), they blossomed into pennant contenders with stars like MVP shortstop Robin Yount, second baseman Paul "The Ignitor" Molitor, and slugging centerfielder Gorman Thomas. Milwaukeeans couldn't have been happier. They had soured on baseball after the Braves left in 1966 for Atlanta, and were reluctant to throw their hearts to a struggling expansion team. But when the Brewers started winning in 1978, the fans flocked to the ballpark.

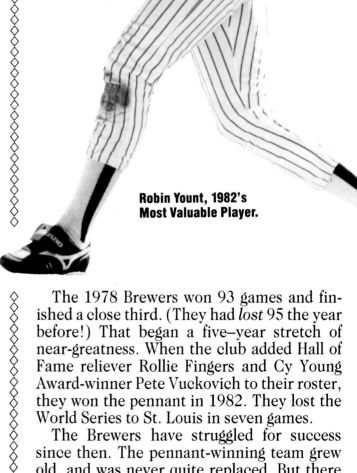

Robin Yount, 1982's Most Valuable Player.

The 1978 Brewers won 93 games and finished a close third. (They had *lost* 95 the year before!) That began a five–year stretch of near-greatness. When the club added Hall of Fame reliever Rollie Fingers and Cy Young Award-winner Pete Vuckovich to their roster, they won the pennant in 1982. They lost the World Series to St. Louis in seven games.

The Brewers have struggled for success since then. The pennant-winning team grew old, and was never quite replaced. But there seems to be hope now for the future. Milwaukee's farm system has produced a number of young, talented pitchers and hitters—enough so that the team may soon be back in the thick of things.

New York Yankees Important Dates:

1903—Frank Farrell and Bill Devery purchase the American League's Baltimore franchise and move it to New York.

1913—Team changes name from Highlanders to Yankees.

1920—Yankees purchase Babe Ruth from Boston.

1923—Yankee Stadium opens and Yankees beat the Giants to win their first World Series.

1927—Ruth hits 60 home runs.

1929—Yankees become the first team to use uniform numbers on a permanent basis.

1934—Yankees purchase Joe DiMaggio.

1941—Joe DiMaggio compiles 56-game hitting streak.

1953—Mickey Mantle hits 565-foot home run in Washington; Yankees win fifth consecutive World Series.

1961—Roger Maris hits 61 home runs.

1973—George Steinbrenner purchases the Yankees.

1975—Billy Martin named manager for the first of five times.

1977—Reggie Jackson hits a record five home runs in the World Series.

Beyond centerfield in majestic Yankee Stadium, between the home and visiting bullpens, stands a memorial park honoring the greatest of all the great New York Yankees. Long lines of fans file through it before every game, past three monuments dedicated to Babe Ruth, Lou Gehrig and Murderers Row manager Miller Huggins, and 17 plaques marking the achievements of Joe DiMaggio, Mickey Mantle, Casey Stengel, Roger Maris, Whitey Ford and other Yankee greats. To the Yankee fans it is a holy place.

These men were not merely sports heroes, they were national heroes. Lou Gehrig was not just the Pride of the Yankees, he was Gary Cooper on the silver screen. Joe DiMaggio wasn't just the Yankee Clipper, he represented the American ideal. Babe Ruth wasn't merely the Sultan of Swat, he *was* America. In World War II, Japanese soldiers would yell, "Death to Babe Ruth!" which they considered, the most insulting thing you could say to an American—and they were generally right.

The Yankees were—and still are—the yardstick against which success in sports is measured. What they accomplished across the eras of Ruth, DiMaggio, Mantle and Reggie Jackson will never be matched. It doesn't matter that the current club isn't winning, or that the Yankees haven't played in the World Series since 1981. To many, there is still no thrill in baseball like the idea of putting on those Yankee pinstripes and trotting onto the diamond in the "House that Ruth Built"—where so many of baseball's heroes have played.

Toronto Blue Jays Important Dates:

1977—Toronto joins the American League.

1983—Blue Jays finish above .500 for the first time.

1985—Blue Jays win their first division title.
1987—George Bell is the team's first All-Star Game starter.
1988—Bell hits three home runs on Opening Day.

No team deserves a trip to the World Series more than the Toronto Blue Jays. Since the mid-1980s, they've come close almost every year. How close?

In 1985, they led Kansas City three games to one in the league playoffs, but then lost the last three games and their chance to play in the Series.

In 1987, they led Detroit by 3½ games with just four games left in the season, but dropped all four by one run and lost the division championship.

In 1988, they finished two games out after rallying from 11½ games back at the All-Star break.

In 1989, the Blue Jays recovered from a 12–24 start to win a tough division race with Baltimore. But then they were steamrollered by Oakland in the playoffs.

That's quite a bit of drama for an expansion team that joined the American League in 1977. But it seems like their time has finally come. The team is full of All-Stars like left-fielder George Bell, first baseman Fred McGriff and pitcher Dave Steib, and the Toronto farm system is brimming with talent. The 1990s may very well be the Jays' decade.

AMERICAN LEAGUE WEST

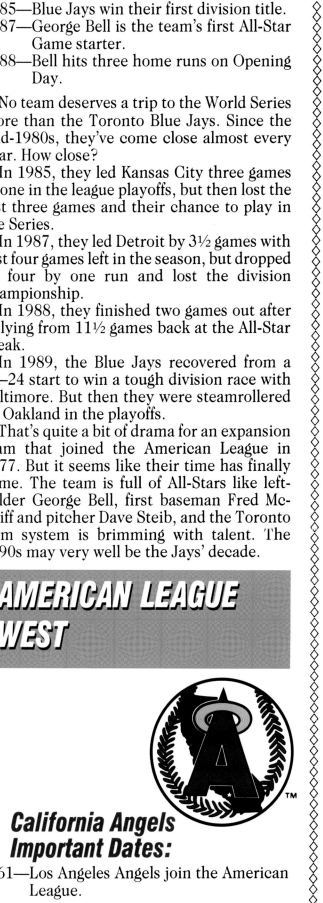

California Angels
Important Dates:

1961—Los Angeles Angels join the American League.

1965—Team is renamed the California Angels.
1966—Anaheim Stadium opens.
1974—Nolan Ryan throws a 100.9 mile-per-hour pitch against Detroit.
1975—Nolan Ryan pitches the fourth of his six no-hitters.
1984—Mike Witt pitches a perfect game against Texas.
1986—Angels win third division title.

How many millions of dollars will owner and former singing cowboy star Gene Autry have to spend before his team finally reaches the World Series? Fifty million? Eighty million? A million billion trillion?

Autry is living proof that money alone can't buy championships. After free agency was created in 1976, Autry took out his checkbook and purchased All-Star outfielders Don Baylor and Joe Rudi, and All-Star second baseman Bobby Grich. When he didn't win that year, he didn't blame his players or his farm system, he just started writing bigger checks. Over the years, he also signed slugging outfielders Reggie Jackson, Chili Davis, Claudell Washington and future Hall of Famer Nolan Ryan, among others, and paid huge sums to retain pitcher Mike Witt, seven-time batting champion Rod Carew and All-Star shortstop Rick Burleson, and kept them from becoming free agents. He has made George Steinbrenner look like small change.

What has all this gotten Autry? Three division titles since entering the league in 1961, but no trips to the World Series. The Angels came within one strike of the Series in 1986, but Boston's Dave Henderson swatted a ninth-inning pitch over the centerfield wall in Anaheim to shatter Autry's dream.

Still, you have to hand it to the guy. Autry hasn't quit. Following the 1989 season, he coughed up $16 million for pitcher Mark Langston, but so far Langston hasn't helped Autry win that pennant. Maybe the old cowboy will at last learn that you can't buy a pennant, you have to earn it.

Chicago White Sox Important Dates:

1901—White Sox become a charter member of the American League.

1910—Comiskey Park opens.

1919—Eight White Sox players, including "Shoeless" Joe Jackson, plot with gamblers to lose the World Series. One year later, the eight are suspended from baseball for life.

1959—White Sox win the pennant for the first time in 40 years.

1985—Tom Seaver wins his 300th game.

The White Sox have never had great hitters. But few teams through the years have produced more brilliant hurlers. There were Hall of Famers Ed Walsh (1.82 lifetime ERA, the lowest in history) and Red Faber (254 wins), and Eddie Cicotte, who was on his way to Cooperstown until his unfortunate involvement with the 1919 "Black Sox" scandal. They were followed over the years by such stars as Billy Pierce, Wilbur Wood, Tommy John, and Hall of Famers Ted Lyons (260 wins) and Early Wynn (300 wins).

Pitching has been the key to nearly all of the Sox's greatest teams. The 1906 squad that upset the rival Chicago Cubs in the World Series was known as the Hitless Wonders. As a team, they batted .230, with a total of seven home runs.

The one champion Sox team that boasted better hitters than pitchers was the notorious 1919 squad, the greatest ballclub in Sox history. That was the team of the great "Shoe-less" Joe Jackson (.356 lifetime average, third highest in history), and three Hall of Famers—catcher Ray Schalk, second baseman Eddie Collins and Faber. Schalk later claimed that if his eight teammates had not taken money to throw the World Series, the Sox, not the Yankees, would have dominated the 1920s.

Today's White Sox are building a team around fine pitching, too. They are hopeful that their young arms will mature by the time the team moves to its new stadium in 1991.

Kansas City Royals Important Dates:

1969—Kansas City Royals join the American League.

1974—Steve Busby pitches his second Royals no-hitter.

1978—Royals win third consecutive division title.

1980—George Brett bats .390.

1985—Royals win the World Series.

1987—Frank White wins his eighth Gold Glove Award.

1989—Bret Saberhagen wins second Cy Young Award.

No expansion team rose as quickly to the top as did the Royals. In 1971, after only three years in the league, they finished in second place. In 1976, they won the first of three consecutive division titles. The Royals placed first or second nine times in 10 years, and won a world championship in 1985. That year, they came from behind to beat their cross-state rivals, the St. Louis Cardinals, in seven games.

The Royals built their team the old-fashioned way, through a productive farm system and smart trades. They skipped the free agent market, and instead created the Baseball Academy, a kind of graduate school for their most promising minor league prospects. George Brett, Bret Saberhagen, Willie Wilson, Mark Gubicza, Kevin Seitzer and Bo Jackson are the pick of their homegrown talent.

Brett, one of the greatest modern hitters, is headed for 3,000 career hits and the Hall of Fame. He batted a remarkable .390 in 1980, the highest average since Ted Williams hit .406 in 1941. Saberhagen had won two Cy Young Awards by the time he was 25.

Following the 1989 season, though, after finishing out of the money four straight years, the Royals decided for the first time to shop for free agents. They signed relief ace Mark Davis, a Cy Young Award winner, and starter Storm Davis. The club is still concentrating on its farm system. Look for them to be at or near the top in the 1990s.

Minnesota Twins Important Dates:

1901—Washington Senators become a charter member of the American League.
1961—Senators move to Minnesota, and are renamed the Twins.
1964—Harmon Killebrew hits 49 home runs and wins his third consecutive home run title.
1965—Twins win the pennant.
1978—Rod Carew wins his sixth batting title in seven years.
1982—Metrodome opens.
1987—Twins win the World Series.

The Twins know hitting even better than Bo does. Over the years, the Twins have been a hitting factory, introducing a new line of .300 machines every few seasons. In the 1920s (when they were the Washington Senators), the club had Hall of Fame outfielders Sam Rice (.322 career batting average) and Goose Goslin (.316).

Later, they produced sluggers such as Hall of Fame third baseman/first baseman Harmon Killebrew (573 home runs) and leftfielder Roy Sievers (318 homers), and high-average hitters such as first baseman and two-time batting champion Mickey Vernon, leftfielder and three-time batting champion Tony Oliva and second baseman and seven-time batting champion Rod Carew.

Today, the Twins have Kirby Puckett and Kent Hrbek, and play in a roofed ballpark known around the league as the "Homerdome."

Unfortunately, the Twins (and earlier, the Senators) haven't always been so knowledgeable about pitching or winning. The Senators had 11 20-game losers between 1901 and 1909. They did develop four remarkable arms—Walter Johnson, Early Wynn, Jim Kaat and Bert Blyleven—but traded all but Johnson during their best years.

As for winning, it was often said of the Washington Senators: "First in war, first in peace and last in the American League." They did better once they moved to Minnesota in 1961 and renamed themselves the Twins. Players such as Killebrew, Oliva and Kaat carried them to a pennant in 1965, and division titles in 1969 and 1970.

Then money entered the picture. Calvin Griffith, the club's longtime owner, couldn't afford the skyrocketing player salaries that resulted from free agency and arbitration, so he began selling and trading his stars. Carew went to California. Slugging outfielder Larry Hisle and relief ace Bill Campbell opted for free agency. The Twins slid back to the bottom of the division, until Griffith sold the club in 1987.

Ironically, the young players such as Puckett, Hrbek and pitcher Frank Viola he acquired to replace his high-priced stars matured that year, and won the World Series.

Money is a factor for new owner Carl

Pohlad, too. In 1989, he traded Viola, and lost relief ace Jeff Reardon to free agency. Once again, the Twins are looking for youngsters to develop and take them to another title.

Oakland A's
Important Dates:

1901—Philadelphia A's become a charter member of American League. Nap Lajoi bats .422.

1913—A's win third World Series in four years.

1930—A's win second straight World Series.

1931—Lefty Grove wins 31 games.

1932—Jimmie Foxx hits 58 home runs.

1950—Connie Mack retires after 50 years as owner/manager of the A's.

1955—A's move to Kansas City.

1968—A's move to Oakland. Catfish Hunter pitches a perfect game against Minnesota.

1974—A's win third consecutive World Series.

1982—Rickey Henderson steals a record 130 bases.

1988—Jose Canseco hits 42 home runs, steals 40 bases.

1989—Oakland sweeps the Giants in the earthquake-delayed World Series.

Could there have been a better team than the 1989 A's? They thundered across the American League West, manhandled the Blue Jays in the league playoffs, and then swept the Giants in the World Series. Jose Canseco, Mark McGwire, Dave Parker and Dave Henderson boomed more home runs than anyone could count; Dave Stewart, Mike Moore, Bob Welch and Dennis Eckersley proved nearly unhittable; and Rickey Henderson turned in a great season's leadoff hitting performance.

As marvelous as they were, though, they might not even rank as the greatest team in A's history.

Consider the team that went to the World Series four times from 1910 to 1914 (as the Philadelphia A's), behind third baseman Frank "Home Run" Baker (four home run titles), second baseman Eddie Collins (3,311 career hits, .333 average), and pitchers Chief Bender (210 wins) and Eddie Plank (327 wins), each of them Hall of Famers. Those A's won three world championships. The 1910 squad led the American League in batting average, slugging average, doubles, triples, fielding average and ERA. Their team ERA, by the way, was 1.79.

Or look at the A's team led by Hall of Famers Jimmie "Double X" Foxx (534 home runs, .325 average), Mickey Cochrane (.320 average), Al Simmons (307 homers, .334 average) and Lefty Grove (300 career wins), that won two world championships and three straight pennants between 1929 and 1931.

Then again, the greatest A's team might have been the 1971–1975 team that won three world championships and five straight division titles, with players such as Hall of Famers Reggie Jackson (563 homers), Catfish Hunter (224 wins) and Rollie Fingers (341 saves).

To be considered the best, the current A's are going to have to keep winning. If the team owners can find the money to keep Henderson, Canseco, McGwire, Stewart and Eckersley, we might see the greatest baseball dynasty in history.

Seattle Mariners
Important Dates:

1977—Seattle Mariners join the American League.

Seattle Mariners Ken Griffey, Jr.

1982—Gaylord Perry wins his 300th game.
1984—Alvin Davis named Rookie of the Year.
1987—Mariners win a club record 78 games (and lose 84).

Have you had the pleasure of watching Ken Griffey, Jr.? He is a sight to behold—as fast as the wind, as strong as the greatest sluggers. He is a young Willie Mays, the greatest hitter Seattle has ever developed. Now, if they can only hold on to him.

Every expansion team endures a few rough years after entering the majors (the Mariners first played in 1977), but Seattle has suffered longer than most. The problem is impatience. Over the years, instead of allowing their young talent to develop, the Mariners have traded it off and have managed to let Mark Langston, Dave Henderson, Danny Tartabull, Phil Bradley, Mike Morgan, Lee Guetterman, Ivan Calderon, Spike Owen, Floyd Bannister and Bill Caudill slip through their hands.

Perhaps there is hope. In 1990, the Mariners rose in the standings, with the help of young players such as rightfielder Greg Briley and third baseman Edgar Martinez. They seem to be following the example set by the Blue Jays, who entered the league the same year. They have stockpiled talented, young players like Griffey, Jr., and are patiently waiting for them to develop. Success may be just around the corner.

Texas Rangers
Important Dates:

1961—A new version of the Washington Senators join the American League.
1972—Senators move to Texas, and are renamed the Rangers.
1973—Rangers pitcher Jim Bibby tosses a no-hitter against Oakland.
1977—Rangers finish 95–68 for second place.
1977—Bert Blyleven tosses a no-hitter against California.

1988—Rangers acquire free agent Nolan Ryan.

The Texas Rangers may be at a turning point in their history. For the first time since they finished second in 1974, they have a talented team. Their lineup is studded with good hitters, among them second baseman Julio Franco, first baseman Rafael Palmeiro, slugging leftfielder Pete Incaviglia, and a budding superstar, rightfielder Ruben Sierra. Their pitching staff includes Hall of Fame–bound Nolan Ryan and Bobby Witt. All of this is good news for a change, for the sad truth is, the Rangers are the only team besides Cleveland and Seattle to go without winning a title since division play began in 1969.

The Rangers' dry spell has actually lasted longer than that. They played as the expansion team Washington Senators from 1961 to 1971, and in those 11 seasons they only once finished higher than sixth. When attendance slumped to 655,000 in 1971, they decided, like many enterprising Americans, that life had to be better in Texas.

A brief period of improvement followed, when Billy Martin managed the new Rangers to a second place finish in 1974. They might have improved even more, had the front office not overreacted, thinking they were just a player or two away from winning it all, and made a flurry of unfortunate trades. Young fireballers Dave Righetti and Ron Darling were among those sent on their way. Soon afterward, the Rangers were struggling again.

But those days are past. The Rangers' new boss is George Bush, Jr., the President's son, and he is breathing new life into a club that is exciting to watch.

SECTION

4

TALKIN'
BASEBALL

ALL-TIME RECORD HOLDERS AND WORLD SERIES WINNERS

Sometimes it seems like we play baseball just so we have some numbers to look at. We memorize batting averages, earned run averages, strikeout totals, stolen base records, the number of pounds Tommy Lasorda has lost and a thousand other stats until we know them like we know the backs of our hands. If someone could make math as much fun as baseball records, we'd be a nation of number crunchers.

The numbers make it easy for us to compare. Is Roger Clemens as good as Nolan Ryan? As Tom Seaver? As Walter Johnson? Does Kirby Puckett hit as well as George Brett? As Rod Carew? As Rogers Hornsby? Who is the better home run hitter—Kevin Mitchell or Rocky Colavito or Hank Greenberg?

Here are the most important records, from 1901 through the end of 1989. See how your favorites compare to the all-time champs.

ALL-TIME SINGLE SEASON LEADERS SINCE 1901— BATTING:

Batting Average			Hits		
1. Rogers Hornsby, 1924	.424		1. George Sisler, 1920		257
2. Nap Lajoie, 1901	.422		2. Bill Terry, 1930		254
3. George Sisler, 1922	.420		2. Lefty O'Doul, 1929		254
3. Ty Cobb, 1911	.420		4. Al Simmons, 1925		253
5. Ty Cobb, 1912	.410		5. Rogers Hornsby, 1922		250
6. Joe Jackson, 1911	.408		5. Chuck Klein, 1930		250
7. George Sisler, 1920	.407		7. Ty Cobb, 1911		248
8. Ted Williams, 1941	.406		8. George Sisler, 1922		246
9. Rogers Hornsby, 1925	.403		9. Babe Herman, 1930		241
9. Harry Heilmann, 1923	.403		9. Heinie Manush, 1928		241

Doubles			Triples		
1. Earl Webb, 1931		67	1. Owen Wilson, 1912		36
2. George Burns, 1926		64	2. Joe Jackson, 1912		26
2. Joe Medwick, 1936		64	2. Sam Crawford, 1914		26
4. Hank Greenberg, 1934		63	2. Kiki Cuyler, 1925		26
5. Paul Waner, 1932		62	5. Tommy Long, 1915		25
6. Charlie Gehringer, 1936		60	5. Larry Doyle, 1911		25
7. Tris Speaker, 1923		59	5. Sam Crawford, 1903		25
7. Chuck Klein, 1930		59	8. Ty Cobb, 1911		24
9. Billy Herman, 1936		57			
9. Billy Herman, 1935		57			

George Sisler.

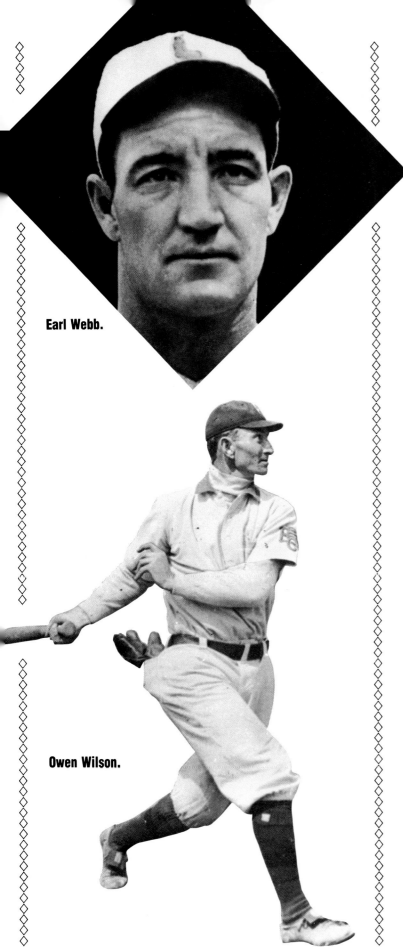

Earl Webb.

Owen Wilson.

Hack Wilson.

Slugging Average

1.	Babe Ruth, 1920	.847
2.	Babe Ruth, 1921	.846
3.	Babe Ruth, 1927	.772
4.	Lou Gehrig, 1927	.765
5.	Babe Ruth, 1923	.764
6.	Rogers Hornsby, 1925	.756
7.	Jimmie Foxx, 1932	.749
8.	Babe Ruth, 1924	.739
9.	Babe Ruth, 1926	.737
10.	Ted Williams, 1941	.735

Extra Base Hits

1.	Babe Ruth, 1921	119
2.	Lou Gehrig, 1927	117
3.	Chuck Klein, 1930	107
4.	Hank Greenberg, 1937	103
4.	Stan Musial, 1948	103
4.	Chuck Klein, 1932	103
7.	Rogers Hornsby, 1922	102
8.	Lou Gehrig, 1930	100
8.	Jimmie Foxx, 1932	100
10.	Babe Ruth, 1920, 1923	99
10.	Hank Greenberg, 1940	99

Home Runs

1.	Roger Maris, 1961	61
2.	Babe Ruth, 1927	60
3.	Babe Ruth, 1921	59
4.	Hank Greenberg, 1938	58
4.	Jimmie Foxx, 1932	58
6.	Hack Wilson, 1930	56
7.	Mickey Mantle, 1961	54
7.	Babe Ruth, 1920	54
7.	Babe Ruth, 1928	54
7.	Ralph Kiner, 1949	54

Runs Batted In

1.	Hack Wilson, 1930	190
2.	Lou Gehrig, 1931	184
3.	Hank Greenberg, 1937	183
4.	Jimmie Foxx, 1938	175
4.	Lou Gehrig, 1927	175
6.	Lou Gehrig, 1930	174
7.	Babe Ruth, 1921	171
8.	Hank Greenberg, 1935	170
8.	Chuck Klein, 1930	170
10.	Jimmie Foxx, 1932	169

Runs

1. Babe Ruth, 1921	177
2. Lou Gehrig, 1936	167
3. Babe Ruth, 1928	163
3. Lou Gehrig, 1931	163
5. Babe Ruth, 1920	158
5. Babe Ruth, 1927	158
5. Chuck Klein, 1930	158
8. Rogers Hornsby, 1929	156
9. Lefty O'Doul, 1929	152
9. Al Simmons, 1930	152
9. Chuck Klein, 1932	152

Total Bases

1. Babe Ruth, 1921	457
2. Rogers Hornsby, 1922	450
3. Lou Gehrig, 1927	447
4. Chuck Klein, 1930	445
5. Jimmie Foxx, 1932	438
6. Stan Musial, 1948	429
7. Hack Wilson, 1930	423
8. Chuck Klein, 1932	420
9. Lou Gehrig, 1930	419
10. Joe DiMaggio, 1937	418

Stolen Bases

1. Rickey Henderson, 1982	130
2. Lou Brock, 1974	118
3. Vince Coleman, 1985	110
4. Vince Coleman, 1987	109
5. Rickey Henderson, 1983	108
6. Vince Coleman, 1986	107
7. Maury Wills, 1962	104
8. Rickey Henderson, 1980	100
9. Ron LeFlore, 1980	97
10. Ty Cobb, 1915	96
10. Omar Moreno, 1980	96

Pinch Hits

1. Jose Morales, 1976	25
2. Rusty Staub, 1983	24
2. Dave Philley, 1961	24
2. Vic Davalillo, 1970	24
5. Wallace Johnson, 1988	22
5. Peanuts Lowrey, 1953	22
5. Sam Leslie, 1932	22
5. Red Schoendienst, 1962	22
8. Smokey Burgess, 1966	21
8. Merv Rettenmund, 1977	21

Bases on Balls

1. Babe Ruth, 1923	170
2. Ted Williams, 1947	162
2. Ted Williams, 1949	162
4. Ted Williams, 1946	156
5. Eddie Yost, 1956	151
6. Eddie Joost, 1949	149
7. Babe Ruth, 1920	148
7. Jimmy Wynn, 1969	148
7. Eddie Stanky, 1945	148
10. Jimmy Sheckard, 1911	147

Strikeouts

1. Bobby Bonds, 1970	189
2. Bobby Bonds, 1969	187
3. Rob Deer, 1987	186
4. Pete Incaviglia, 1986	185
5. Mick Schmidt, 1975	180
6. Rob Deer, 1986	179
7. Jose Canseco, 1986	175
7. Gorman Thomas, 1979	175
7. Dave Nicholson, 1963	175
10. Jim Presley, 1986	172
10. Bo Jackson, 1989	172

Dutch Leonard.

ALL-TIME SINGLE SEASON LEADERS SINCE 1901— PITCHING:

Wins

1. Jack Chesbro, 1904	41
2. Ed Walsh, 1908	40
3. Christy Mathewson, 1908	37
4. Walter Johnson, 1913	36
5. Joe McGinnity, 1904	35
6. Joe Wood, 1912	34
7. Cy Young, 1901	33
7. Grover Alexander, 1916	33
7. Christy Mathewson, 1904	33
10. Cy Young, 1902	32

Earned Run Average

1. Dutch Leonard, 1914	1.01
2. Mordecai Brown, 1906	1.04
3. Walter Johnson, 1913	1.09
4. Bob Gibson, 1968	1.12
5. Christy Mathewson, 1909	1.14
6. Jack Pfeister, 1907	1.15
7. Addie Joss, 1908	1.16
8. Carl Lundgren, 1907	1.17
9. Grover Alexander, 1915	1.22
10. Cy Young, 1908	1.26

Strikeouts

1. Nolan Ryan, 1973	383
2. Sandy Koufax, 1965	382
3. Nolan Ryan, 1974	367
4. Rube Waddell, 1904	349
5. Bob Feller, 1946	348
6. Nolan Ryan, 1977	341
7. Nolan Ryan, 1972	329
8. Nolan Ryan, 1976	327
9. Sam McDowell, 1965	325
10. Sandy Koufax, 1966	317

Shutouts

1. Grover Alexander, 1916	16
2. Bob Gibson, 1968	13
2. Jack Coombs, 1910	13
4. Grover Alexander, 1915	12
4. Christy Mathewson, 1908	12
5. Dean Chance, 1964	11
5. Walter Johnson, 1913	11
5. Sandy Koufax, 1963	11
5. Ed Walsh, 1908	11

Jack Chesbro.

Grover Cleveland Alexander.

Hits per 9 Innings

1. Nolan Ryan, 1972	5.26
2. Luis Tiant, 1968	5.30
3. Ed Reulbach, 1906	5.33
4. Jim Hearn, 1950	5.64
5. Carl Lundgren, 1907	5.65
6. Dutch Leonard, 1914	5.70
7. Sid Fernandez, 1985	5.71
8. Tommy Byrne, 1949	5.74
9. Dave McNally, 1968	5.77
10. Sandy Koufax, 1965	5.79

Saves

1. Dave Righetti, 1986	46
2. Bruce Sutter, 1984	45
2. Dan Quisenberry, 1983	45
2. Dennis Eckersley, 1988	45
5. Mark Davis, 1989	44
5. Dan Quisenberry, 1984	44
7. Jeff Reardon, 1988	42
8. Jeff Reardon, 1985	41
9. Steve Bedrosian, 1987	40
10. John Franco, 1988	39

ALL-TIME CAREER LEADERS SINCE 1901—BATTING:

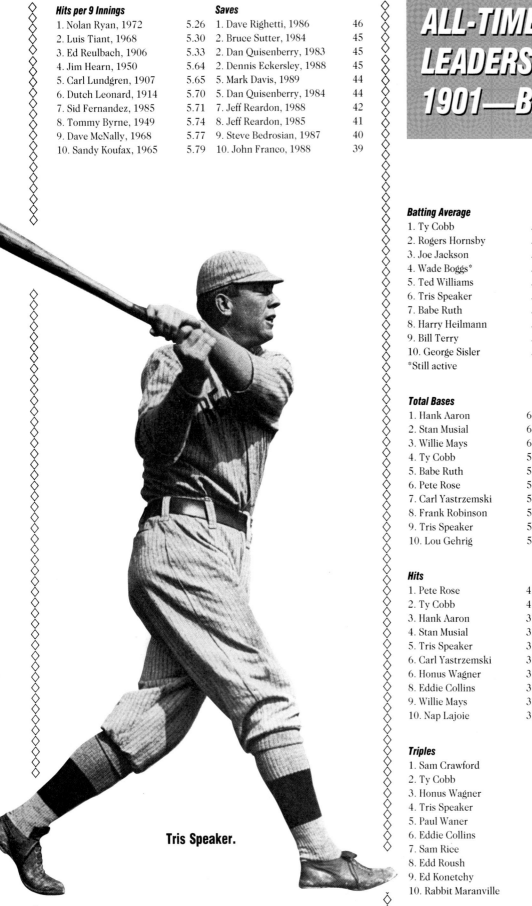

Tris Speaker.

Batting Average

1. Ty Cobb	.367
2. Rogers Hornsby	.358
3. Joe Jackson	.356
4. Wade Boggs*	.352
5. Ted Williams	.344
6. Tris Speaker	.344
7. Babe Ruth	.342
8. Harry Heilmann	.342
9. Bill Terry	.341
10. George Sisler	.340
*Still active	

Slugging Average

1. Babe Ruth	.690
2. Ted Williams	.634
3. Lou Gehrig	.632
4. Jimmie Foxx	.609
5. Hank Greenberg	.605
6. Joe DiMaggio	.579
7. Rogers Hornsby	.577
8. Johnny Mize	.562
9. Stan Musial	.559
10. Willie Mays	.557

Total Bases

1. Hank Aaron	6,856
2. Stan Musial	6,134
3. Willie Mays	6,066
4. Ty Cobb	5,863
5. Babe Ruth	5,793
6. Pete Rose	5,752
7. Carl Yastrzemski	5,539
8. Frank Robinson	5,373
9. Tris Speaker	5,104
10. Lou Gehrig	5,059

Games

1. Pete Rose	3,562
2. Carl Yastrzemski	3,308
3. Hank Aaron	3,298
4. Ty Cobb	3,034
5. Stan Musial	3,026
6. Willie Mays	2,992
7. Rusty Staub	2,951
8. Brooks Robinson	2,896
9. Al Kaline	2,834
10. Eddie Collins	2,826

Hits

1. Pete Rose	4,256
2. Ty Cobb	4,191
3. Hank Aaron	3,771
4. Stan Musial	3,630
5. Tris Speaker	3,515
6. Carl Yastrzemski	3,419
6. Honus Wagner	3,418
8. Eddie Collins	3,311
9. Willie Mays	3,283
10. Nap Lajoie	3,244

Doubles

1. Tris Speaker	792
2. Pete Rose	746
3. Stan Musial	725
4. Ty Cobb	724
5. Nap Lajoie	658
6. Carl Yastrzemski	646
7. Honus Wagner	643
8. Hank Aaron	624
9. Paul Waner	603
10. Charlie Gehringer	574

Triples

1. Sam Crawford	312
2. Ty Cobb	297
3. Honus Wagner	252
4. Tris Speaker	223
5. Paul Waner	190
6. Eddie Collins	187
7. Sam Rice	184
8. Edd Roush	182
9. Ed Konetchy	181
10. Rabbit Maranville	177

Home Runs

1. Hank Aaron	755
2. Babe Ruth	714
3. Willie Mays	660
4. Frank Robinson	586
5. Harmon Killebrew	573
6. Reggie Jackson	563
7. Mike Schmidt	548
8. Mickey Mantle	536
9. Jimmie Foxx	534
10. Ted Williams	521

Sam Crawford.

Runs Batted In		Runs	
1. Hank Aaron	2,297	1. Ty Cobb	2,245
2. Babe Ruth	2,211	2. Babe Ruth	2,174
3. Lou Gehrig	1,990	2. Hank Aaron	2,174
4. Ty Cobb	1,961	4. Pete Rose	2,165
5. Stan Musial	1,951	5. Willie Mays	2,062
6. Jimmie Foxx	1,921	6. Stan Musial	1,949
7. Willie Mays	1,903	7. Lou Gehrig	1,888
8. Mel Ott	1,861	8. Tris Speaker	1,881
9. Carl Yastrzemski	1,844	9. Mel Ott	1,859
10. Ted Williams	1,839	10. Frank Robinson	1,829

Bases on Balls		Strikeouts	
1. Babe Ruth	2,056	1. Reggie Jackson	2,597
2. Ted Williams	2,019	2. Willie Stargell	1,936
3. Joe Morgan	1,865	3. Mike Schmidt	1,883
4. Carl Yastrzemski	1,845	4. Tony Perez	1,867
5. Mickey Mantle	1,734	5. Dave Kingman	1,816
6. Mel Ott	1,708	6. Bobby Bonds	1,757
7. Eddie Yost	1,614	7. Lou Brock	1,730
8. Darrell Evans	1,605	8. Mickey Mantle	1,710
9. Stan Musial	1,599	9. Harmon Killebrew	1,699
10. Pete Rose	1,566	10. Lee May	1,570
		10. Dwight Evans*	1,570

*Still active

Stolen Bases		Pinch Hits	
1. Lou Brock	938	1. Manny Mota	150
2. Ty Cobb	892	2. Smokey Burgess	145
3. Rickey Henderson*	871	3. Greg Gross	143
4. Eddie Collins	743	4. Jose Morales	123
5. Max Carey	738	5. Jerry Lynch	116
6. Honus Wagner	703	6. Red Lucas	114
7. Joe Morgan	689	7. Steve Braun	113
8. Bert Campaneris	649	8. Terry Crowley	108
9. Willie Wilson*	588	9. Gates Brown	107
10. Maury Wills	586	10. Mike Lum	103

*Still active

Lou Brock.

ALL-TIME CAREER LEADERS SINCE 1901—PITCHING:

Wins
1. Cy Young	511
2. Walter Johnson	416
3. Christy Mathewson	373
3. Grover Alexander	373
5. Warren Spahn	363
6. Steve Carlton	329
7. Eddie Plank	327
8. Don Sutton	324
9. Phil Niekro	318
10. Gaylord Perry	314

Earned Run Average
1. Ed Walsh	1.82
2. Addie Joss	1.88
3. Mordecai Brown	2.06
4. Christy Mathewson	2.13
5. Rube Waddell	2.16
6. Walter Johnson	2.17
7. Orval Overall	2.24
8. Ed Reulbach	2.28
9. Jim Scott	2.32
10. Eddie Plank	2.34

Games
1. Hoyt Wilhelm	1,070
2. Kent Tekulve	1,050
3. Lindy McDaniel	987
4. Rollie Fingers	944
5. Gene Garber	931
6. Cy Young	906
7. Sparky Lyle	899
8. Jim Kaat	898
9. Don McMahon	874
10. Phil Niekro	864
*Still active	

Innings Pitched
1. Cy Young	7,356
2. Walter Johnson	5,923
3. Phil Niekro	5,403
4. Gaylord Perry	5,351
5. Don Sutton	5,280
6. Warren Spahn	5,244
7. Steve Carlton	5,217
8. Grover Alexander	5,189
9. Nolan Ryan*	4,787
10. Tom Seaver	4,783

Rollie Fingers.

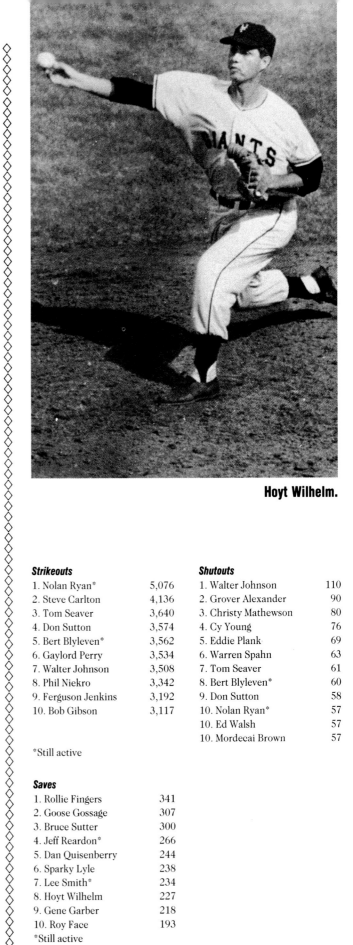

Hoyt Wilhelm.

Strikeouts
1. Nolan Ryan*	5,076
2. Steve Carlton	4,136
3. Tom Seaver	3,640
4. Don Sutton	3,574
5. Bert Blyleven*	3,562
6. Gaylord Perry	3,534
7. Walter Johnson	3,508
8. Phil Niekro	3,342
9. Ferguson Jenkins	3,192
10. Bob Gibson	3,117

*Still active

Shutouts
1. Walter Johnson	110
2. Grover Alexander	90
3. Christy Mathewson	80
4. Cy Young	76
5. Eddie Plank	69
6. Warren Spahn	63
7. Tom Seaver	61
8. Bert Blyleven*	60
9. Don Sutton	58
10. Nolan Ryan*	57
10. Ed Walsh	57
10. Mordecai Brown	57

Saves
1. Rollie Fingers	341
2. Goose Gossage	307
3. Bruce Sutter	300
4. Jeff Reardon*	266
5. Dan Quisenberry	244
6. Sparky Lyle	238
7. Lee Smith*	234
8. Hoyt Wilhelm	227
9. Gene Garber	218
10. Roy Face	193
*Still active	

WORLD SERIES RESULTS YEAR BY YEAR:

	Winner	Loser	Score
1903	Boston Red Sox (A.L.)	Pittsburgh Pirates (N.L.)	5–3
1904	(No World Series)		
1905	New York Giants (N.L.)	Philadelphia Athletics (A.L.)	4–1
1906	Chicago White Sox (A.L.)	Chicago Cubs (N.L.)	4–2
1907	Chicago Cubs (N.L.)	Detroit Tigers (A.L.)	4–0
1908	Chicago Cubs (N.L.)	Detroit Tigers (A.L.)	4–1
1909	Pittsburgh Pirates (N.L.)	Detroit Tigers (A.L.)	4–3
1910	Philadelphia Athletics (A.L.)	Chicago Cubs (N.L.)	4–1
1911	Philadelphia Athletics (A.L.)	New York Giants (N.L.)	4–2
1912	Boston Red Sox (A.L.)	New York Giants (N.L.)	4–3
1913	Philadelphia Athletics (A.L.)	New York Giants (N.L.)	4–1
1914	Boston Braves (N.L.)	Philadelphia Athletics (A.L.)	4–0
1915	Boston Red Sox (A.L.)	Philadelphia Phillies (N.L.)	4–1
1916	Boston Red Sox (A.L.)	Brooklyn Dodgers (N.L.)	4–1
1917	Chicago White Sox (A.L.)	New York Giants (N.L.)	4–2
1918	Boston Red Sox (A.L.)	Chicago Cubs (N.L.)	4–2
1919	Cincinnati Reds (N.L.)	Chicago White Sox (A.L.)	5–3
1920	Cleveland Indians (A.L.)	Brooklyn Dodgers (N.L.)	5–2
1921	New York Giants (N.L.)	New York Yankees (A.L.)	5–3
1922	New York Giants (N.L.)	New York Yankees (A.L.)	4–0
1923	New York Yankees (A.L.)	New York Giants (N.L.)	4–2
1924	Washington Senators (A.L.)	New York Giants (N.L.)	4–3
1925	Pittsburgh Pirates (N.L.)	Washington Senators (A.L.)	4–3
1926	St. Louis Cardinals (N.L.)	New York Yankees (A.L.)	4–3
1927	New York Yankees (A.L.)	Pittsburgh Pirates (N.L.)	4–0
1928	New York Yankees (A.L.)	St. Louis Cardinals (N.L.)	4–0
1929	Philadelphia Athletics (A.L.)	Chicago Cubs (N.L.)	4–1
1930	Philadelphia Athletics (A.L.)	St. Louis Cardinals (N.L.)	4–2
1931	St. Louis Cardinals (N.L.)	Philadelphia Athletics (A.L.)	4–3
1932	New York Yankees (A.L.)	Chicago Cubs (N.L.)	4–0
1933	New York Giants (N.L.)	Washington Senators (A.L.)	4–1
1934	St. Louis Cardinals (N.L.)	Detroit Tigers (A.L.)	4–3
1935	Detroit Tigers (A.L.)	Chicago Cubs (N.L.)	4–2
1936	New York Yankees (A.L.)	New York Giants (N.L.)	4–2
1937	New York Yankees (A.L.)	New York Giants (N.L.)	4–1
1938	New York Yankees (A.L.)	Chicago Cubs (N.L.)	4–0
1939	New York Yankees (A.L.)	Cincinnati Reds (N.L.)	4–0
1940	Cincinnati Reds (N.L.)	Detroit Tigers (A.L.)	4–3
1941	New York Yankees (A.L.)	Brooklyn Dodgers (N.L.)	4–1
1942	St. Louis Cardinals (N.L.)	New York Yankees (A.L.)	4–1
1943	New York Yankees (A.L.)	St. Louis Cardinals (N.L.)	4–1
1944	St. Louis Cardinals (N.L.)	St. Louis Browns (A.L.)	4–2
1945	Detroit Tigers (A.L.)	Chicago Cubs (N.L.)	4–3
1946	St. Louis Cardinals (N.L.)	Boston Red Sox (A.L.)	4–3
1947	New York Yankees (A.L.)	Brooklyn Dodgers (N.L.)	4–3
1948	Cleveland Indians (A.L.)	Boston Braves (N.L.)	4–2
1949	New York Yankees (A.L.)	Brooklyn Dodgers (N.L.)	4–1

	Winner	Loser	Score
1950	New York Yankees (A.L.)	Philadelphia Phillies (N.L.)	4–0
1951	New York Yankees (A.L.)	New York Giants (N.L.)	4–2
1952	New York Yankees (A.L.)	Brooklyn Dodgers (N.L.)	4–3
1953	New York Yankees (A.L.)	Brooklyn Dodgers (N.L.)	4–2
1954	New York Giants (N.L.)	Cleveland Indians (A.L.)	4–0
1955	Brooklyn Dodgers (N.L.)	New York Yankees (A.L.)	4–3
1956	New York Yankees (A.L.)	Brooklyn Dodgers (N.L.)	4–3
1957	Milwaukee Braves (N.L.)	New York Yankees (A.L.)	4–3
1958	New York Yankees (A.L.)	Milwaukee Braves (N.L.)	4–3
1959	Los Angeles Dodgers (N.L.)	Chicago White Sox (A.L.)	4–2
1960	Pittsburgh Pirates (N.L.)	New York Yankees (A.L.)	4–3
1961	New York Yankees (A.L.)	Cincinnati Reds (N.L.)	4–1
1962	New York Yankees (A.L.)	San Francisco Giants (N.L.)	4–3
1963	Los Angeles Dodgers (N.L.)	New York Yankees (A.L.)	4–0
1964	St. Louis Cardinals (N.L.)	New York Yankees (A.L.)	4–3
1965	Los Angeles Dodgers (N.L.)	Minnesota Twins (A.L.)	4–3
1966	Baltimore Orioles (A.L.)	Los Angeles Dodgers (N.L.)	4–0
1967	St. Louis Cardinals (N.L.)	Boston Red Sox (A.L.)	4–3
1968	Detroit Tigers (A.L.)	St. Louis Cardinals (N.L.)	4–3
1969	New York Yankees (N.L.)	Baltimore Orioles (A.L.)	4–1
1970	Baltimore Orioles (A.L.)	Cincinnati Reds (N.L.)	4–1
1971	Pittsburgh Pirates (N.L.)	Baltimore Orioles (A.L.)	4–3
1972	Oakland A's (A.L.)	Cincinnati Reds (N.L.)	4–3
1973	Oakland A's (A.L.)	New York Mets (N.L.)	4–3
1974	Oakland A's (A.L.)	Los Angeles Dodgers (N.L.)	4–1
1975	Cincinnati Reds (N.L.)	Boston Red Sox (A.L.)	4–3
1976	Cincinnati Reds (N.L.)	New York Yankees (A.L.)	4–0
1977	New York Yankees (A.L.)	Los Angeles Dodgers (N.L.)	4–2
1978	New York Yankees (A.L.)	Los Angeles Dodgers (N.L.)	4–2
1979	Pittsburgh Pirates (N.L.)	Baltimore Orioles (A.L.)	4–3
1980	Philadelphia Phillies (N.L.)	Kansas City Royals (A.L.)	4–2
1981	Los Angeles Dodgers (N.L.)	New York Yankees (A.L.)	4–2
1982	St. Louis Cardinals (N.L.)	Milwaukee Brewers (A.L.)	4–3
1983	Baltimore Orioles (A.L.)	Philadelphia Phillies (N.L.)	4–1
1984	Detroit Tigers (A.L.)	San Diego (N.L.)	4–1
1985	Kansas City Royals (A.L.)	St. Louis Cardinals (N.L.)	4–3
1986	New York Mets (N.L.)	Boston Red Sox (A.L.)	4–3
1987	Minnesota Twins (A.L.)	St. Louis Cardinals (N.L.)	4–3
1988	Los Angeles Dodgers (N.L.)	Oakland A's (A.L.)	4–1
1989	Oakland A's (A.L.)	San Francisco Giants (N.L.)	4–0

CHAPTER 11

BASEBALL NICKNAMES

Do you think the names you call your friends are goofy? Baseball players are the *kings* of goofy. It's one thing for Theodore Cleaver to spend his childhood as the Beaver, but what can you say about a grown man who goes happily through life as Bow Wow Arft or Hill Billy Bildilli? The following is a list of the wackiest and weirdest major league nicknames.

Joe "Wagon Tongue" Adams
Luke "Old Aches and Pains" Appling
Hank "Bow Wow" Arft
Abraham Lincoln "Sweetbreads" Bailey
Tom "Rattlesnake" Baker
Charles "Lady" Baldwin
Desmond "Desperate" Beatty
Walter "Boom-Boom" Beck
Joe "Bananas" Benes
Claude "Admiral" Berry
"Jittery Joe" Berry
Emil "Hill Billy" Bildilli
Dennis "Oil Can" Boyd
Joe "Goobers" Bratcher
Anthony "Bunny" Brief
Frank "Turkeyfoot" Brower
"Glass Arm Eddie" Brown
Mordecai "Three Finger" Brown
Tommy "Buckshot" Brown
"Black Jack" Burdock
"Parisian Bob" Caruthers

Emil "Hill Billy" Bildilli.

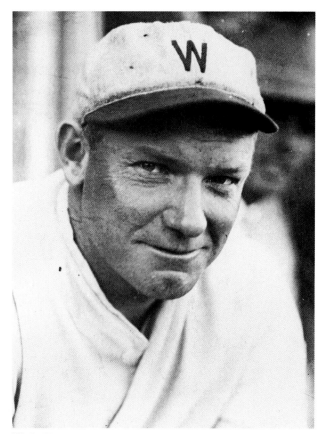

Nick "Tomato Face" Cullop.

Fred "Bootnose" Hofmann
Joe "Ubbo Ubbo" Hornung
Elmer "Herky Jerky" Horton
Frank "Pig" House
William "Dummy" Hoy
Al "The Mad Hungarian" Hrabosky
Jim "Catfish" Hunter
Joe "Poodles" Hutcheson
Al "Bear Tracks" Javery
Walter "Big Train" Johnson
Davy "Kangaroo" Jones
Willie "Puddin' Head" Jones
George "Highpockets" Kelly
"Twilight Ed" Killian
Ellis "Old Folks" Kinder
Bill "Little Eva" Lange
"Tobacco Chewin' Johnny" Lanning
Frank "Pot" LaPorte
Don "Footsie" Lenhardt
Ed "Eggie" Lennox
Jeffrey "Penitentiary Face" Leonard

"Crooning Joe" Cascarella
Charles "The Old Roman" Comiskey
Duff "Sir Richard" Cooley
Pat "Whopps" Creeden
Nick "Tomato Face" Cullop
Andre "Hawk" Dawson
Roger "Peaceful Valley" Denzer
Joe "The Yankee Clipper" DiMaggio
George "Pea Soup" Dumont
Leo "The Lip" Durocher
Chet "Spot" Falk
Bob "Warrior" Friend
Del "Sheriff" Gainor
"Diry Al" Gallagher
Lou "The Iron Horse" Gehrig
Paul "Gorilla" Gilliford
Len "Meow" Gilmore
Frank "Inch" Gleich
Joe "Gabber" Glenn
Burleigh "Ol' Stubblebeard" Grimes
Don "Jeep" Heffner
Tommy "Old Reliable" Henrich
"Still Bill" Hill
Chuck "Iron Hands" Hiller

Al "The Mad Hungarian" Hrabosky.

Jeffrey "Penitentiary Face" Leonard.

Jim "Grasshopper" Lillie
Sal "The Barber" Maglie
Clarence "Cuddles" Marshall
Pepper "The Wild Hoss of the Osage" Martin
Willie "Say Hey" Mays
Pryor "Humpy" McElveen
Frank "Beauty" McGowan
John "Little Napoleon" McGraw
Eric "Boob" McNair
Benny "Earache" Meyer
Russ "The Mad Monk" Meyer
Johnny "The Big Cat" Mize
John "The Count" Montefusco
Gene "Blue Goose" Moore
Ray "Farmer" Moore
Tom "Plowboy" Morgan
"Jughandle Johnny" Morrison
Hugh "Losing Pitcher" Mulcahy
Jack "Peach Pie" O'Connor
"Orator Jim" O'Rourke
"Voiceless Time" O'Rourke
Eddie "Baldy" Palmer
Camilo "Little Patato" Pascual
Tony "Doggie" Perez
John "Pretzels" Pezzullo
Fred "Dandelion" Pfeffer
Dick "Twitchy" Porter
Phil "Grandmother" Powers
Frank "Truckhorse" Pratt
Wellington "Wimpy" Quinn
James "Icicle" Reeder
Phil "The Vulture" Regan
Lee "Bee Bee" Richard
"Pigtail Billy" Riley
Claude "Little All Right" Ritchey
Lew "Old Dog" Ritter
Phil "Scooter" Rizzuto
"Raw Meat Bill" Rodgers
Johnny "Honey" Romano
Johnny "The Crabapple Comet" Rucker
Gene "Half-Pint" Rye
Joe "Horse Belly" Sargent
Harry "Silk Stocking" Schafer
Frank "Wildfire" Schulte
Bill "Blab" Schwartz
George "Twinkletoes" Selkirk
Ernest "Mule" Shirley
Edwin "Duke" Snider
Moe "The Rabbi of Swat" Solomon
Bob "Spook" Speake
Allyn "Fish Hook" Stout
Alan "Inky" Strange

Dick "Dr. Strangeglove" Stuart
Harvey "Suds" Sutherland
Harry "Ducky" Swan
Ed "Dimples" Tate
Charles "Pussy" Tebeau
George "White Wings" Tebeau
Oliver "Patsy" Tebeau

Walter "No-Neck" Williams.

Rollie "Bunions" Zeider.

Ledell "Cannonball" Titcomb
Harry "Bird Eye" Truby
Cecil "Turkey" Tyson
William "Peek-A-Boo" Veach
Leon "Daddy Wags" Wagner
Fred "Mysterious" Walker
Lloyd "Little Poison" Waner
Paul "Big Poison" Waner
Walter "Mother" Watson
Will "Whoop-La" White
Jimmy "Buttons" Williams
Mitch "Wild Thing" Williams
Ted "The Splendid Splinter" Williams
Walter "No-Neck" Williams
Charlie "Swamp Baby" Wilson
William "Chicken" Wolf
Clarence "Yam" Yaryan
Jim "Grapefruit" Yeargin
Moses "Chief" Yellowhorse
Rollie "Bunions" Zeider
Bill "Goober" Zuber
Frank "Noodles" Zupo

GLOSSARY

Artificial turf   A man-made surface, such as Astro-turf, used instead of grass on the playing field.

At bat   An official turn at the plate.

Balk   An illegal and deceptive move made by the pitcher. It is a change in the pitcher's normal delivery designed to deceive a base runner. Penalty: each runner advances one base.

Ball   A pitch thrown outside the strike zone.

Base on balls   Four balls pitched out of the strike zone. Also known as a "walk." Batter advances to first base.

Batter's box   The rectangular areas to the left and right of home plate where batters must stand while batting.

Batting order   The official order in which players come to bat.

Beanball   A high, inside pitch intentionally thrown at the batter's head.

Blooper   A short fly ball to the outfield.

Bullpen   An area off the playing field where relief pitchers warm up.

Bunt   A soft hit resulting from the batter simply holding the bat out and letting the ball hit it, rather than from swinging the bat.

Catcher's box   The rectangular area behind home plate where the catcher must remain until a pitch is delivered.

Catcher's signal   The sign a catcher flashes to the pitcher with his fingers to indicate the type of pitch the catcher wants the pitcher to throw.

Changeup   A pitch thrown at a slower-than-normal speed, in an effort to throw off the batter's timing. The pitch is thrown with the same motion used for a fastball.

Curveball   A pitch thrown by a righthander that breaks down and to the left, or a pitch thrown by a lefthander that breaks down and to the right.

Cutoff   A ball, generally thrown by an outfielder, that is intercepted by an infielder, who then relays the ball to the plate or another base.

Cutoff man   The player who makes the cutoff, generally the shortstop or second baseman.

Double play   A single defensive play that results in two outs.

Dugout   The area where players sit when they are not at bat, on base, or playing in the field.

Earned run   A run scored without any errors, passed balls, obstructions or other interferences.

Earned run average (ERA)   A pitching statistic determined by multiplying the number of earned runs a pitcher has given up by nine, and then dividing by the number of innings pitched. It is one measure of a pitcher's effectiveness.

Error   A fielding misplay or wild throw that allows the batter to reach base, or a runner to advance a base.

Extra-base hit   A double, triple or home run.

Force-out   A play in which a fielder who has the ball retires a runner by tagging the base the runner is proceeding to before the runner arrives there. Force-outs apply only with a runner on first, runners on first and second, runners on first, second and third, or runners on first and third (in this situation, only the man on first can be forced).

Foul ball   A batted ball that lands outside the foul lines before reaching first or third base, or that first touches the ground outside the foul lines beyond first or third.

Full count   When there are three balls and two strikes on the batter.

Grand slam   A home run hit with the bases loaded.

Guess hitter   A batter who tries to guess the type of pitch the pitcher intends to throw, rather than simply reacting to the ball.

Hit-and-run   A strategic play that calls for the batter to swing as the baserunner breaks for the next base. For the play to work best, the batter must hit the ball on the ground, no matter where the pitch is thrown.

Hit batter   A batter hit by a pitched ball. The batter is awarded first base.

Home run   A four-base hit.

Infield   The section of the field where the catcher, pitcher, first baseman, second baseman, shortstop and third baseman stand.

Inning   A segment of a baseball game in which each team bats until it makes three outs. There are nine innings in a regulation game.

Knuckleball   A pitch that is thrown by gripping the ball with the fingernails or first knuckles of the throwing hand. A knuckleball has very little spin, and may break in any direction.

Lead   The distance a runner stands away from the base.

Leadoff man   The first batter in the official batting order.

Line drive   A hard-hit ball that travels parallel to the ground, rather than in a rainbow-like path.

Lineup   Same as the batting order.

Mound   The raised area where the pitcher stands to pitch. The pitcher's rubber is set in the top of the mound, 60 feet, 6 inches from the plate.

On-deck circle   The area in foul territory where the next batter stands or kneels as he waits to hit.

One-hopper   A ground ball that reaches a fielder after hitting the ground just once.

Opposite field   The part of the field that is opposite the side of the plate from which a batter hits. Leftfield is the opposite field for a lefthanded batter; rightfield, for a righthanded batter.

Outfield   The area of the field beyond the infield where the centerfielder, leftfielder and right-fielder stand.

Passed ball   A pitch that gets past the catcher, and that the catcher should have caught or blocked.

Pickoff   A sudden throw by the pitcher or the catcher to an infielder in an effort to catch a runner off base.

Pinch hitter   A batter who substitutes for the scheduled batter in the official lineup.

Pinch runner   A runner who substitutes for a runner already occupying a base.

Pitching rotation   The order in which a team's starting pitchers start ballgames. Most teams use a five-man pitching rotation.

Pitching staff   The entire group of pitchers that pitch for a particular team. Most staffs consist of 10 pitchers.

Pitchout   A ball deliberately pitched wide of the strike zone so the batter can't reach it. Pitch-outs are generally used so the catcher has a better chance to catch a runner who is trying to steal a base.

Power hitter   A batter capable of hitting numerous home runs.

Pull hitter   A righthanded batter who hits mostly to leftfield or a lefthanded batter who hits mostly to rightfield.

Relay man   Same as cutoff man.

Relief pitcher   A pitcher who enters the game in place of a previous pitcher.

Rookie   A first-year player.

Run batted in (RBI)   A statistic that credits a batter for driving in a run with a hit, a sacrifice, a base on balls or by being hit with a pitch.

Rundown   A play in which a runner is caught between two fielders and tagged out.

Sacrifice   A bunt that advances a base runner at the expense of the batter who is thrown out at first base.

Sacrifice fly   A fly to the outfield that scores a base runner after the ball is caught.

Save   A statistic that credits a relief pitcher who enters a game with his team ahead, and preserves a victory.

Screwball   A pitch that breaks in the opposite direction of a curveball. Thrown by a right-hander, it will break in on a righthanded batter. Thrown by a lefthander, it will break in on a lefthanded batter.

Shutout   A game in which the losing team does not score.

Single   A hit where the batter reaches first base safely.

Singles hitter   A batter with little power.

Slide   A dive, either headfirst or feet first, toward a base.

Slider A pitch that looks like a fastball, but breaks sharply as it crosses the plate.

Slump An extended period of poor performance for a hitter, pitcher, fielder, or club.

Spitball An illegal pitch in which a moist substance is added to the ball to make it drop or curve.

Squeeze play A play in which the batter bunts in an attempt to drive in a runner from third.

Stepping in the bucket When a batter steps away from home plate with his front foot as he is swinging. Stepping in the bucket can lead to a slump.

Stolen base A play in which the base runner advances a base as the pitcher is throwing the ball to the plate.

Stretch position The motion a pitcher uses with men on base. It is a two-part motion interrupted by a pause. Its purpose is to keep runners from taking big leads. When pitching from the stretch, a pitcher's back foot is parallel to, rather than across, the rubber.

Strike A pitch thrown in the strike zone that the batter lets pass, or a pitch the batter swings at and misses, or fouls off with fewer than two strikes.

Strikeout When a batter is retired on three strikes.

Switch-hitter A batter who can hit both right-handed and lefthanded.

Tag To retire a runner by touching him with the ball or a glove holding the ball.

Tagging up Returning to a base until a fly ball is caught, and then running to the next base.

Take To let a pitch go by without swinging.

About the Author

Ron Berler's work has appeared in *Sports Illustrated, Playboy, Outside* and *Chicago* magazines. He was a crackerjack shortstop until middle age turned him into a no-range third baseman. Now he manages Little Leaguers who breeze the ball by him at will. He teaches sports journalism at Northwestern University and lives in a Chicago suburb.